LIFE SKILLS BOOK FOR TEENS

LiFE SKiLLS BOOK →FOR← TEENS

EVERYTHING YOU NEED TO KNOW TO BE MORE INDEPENDENT

MAUREEN STILES

callisto
publishing
an imprint of Sourcebooks

Art Director: Angela Navarra & Erik Jacobsen

Art Producer: Stacey Stambaugh

Editor: Annie Choi

Production Editor: Rachel Taenzler

Production Manager: Martin Worthington

Published by Callisto Publishing LLC C/O Sourcebooks LLC
P.O. Box 4410, Naperville, Illinois 60567-4410
(630) 961-3900
callistopublishing.com

Printed and bound in the United States of America.
VP 10 9 8 7 6 5 4 3 2 1

To Mark, Mac, Drew, and Reed,
my partners in crime, inspiration,
and greatest joy.

CONTENTS

HOW TO USE THIS BOOK

Welcome to *Life Skills Book for Teens*! You're taking the first step to becoming an adult by seeking information. That's huge! Adulting is just that—a series of steps. You won't become an adult overnight, but my goal with this book is to make the journey easier.

My name is Maureen Stiles. I am a writer, a published author, and a mom with over two decades of parenting experience. I have successfully launched three teens into adulthood and will draw from that experience to help you gain independence, too.

Becoming an adult can be a confusing process. One minute you're shouting, "I can do this," and the next you're wondering, "What am I doing?" I remember that roller-coaster ride of emotions and saw it in my own kids as well. This book will be your guardrail through the dips and turns of burgeoning adulthood. It can also be an ongoing reference as you encounter new situations and circumstances. You may be tempted to skip over familiar topics.

Although you may already be familiar with them, take another look and dig deeper. Understanding the why behind these suggestions will help you make better decisions.

One piece of general advice about decisions: Don't assume, ask! Sometimes, you might feel tempted to forge ahead without the tools and knowledge to make educated choices. Some of my kids' biggest mistakes were a result of trying to handle situations beyond their scope of experience by themselves. Asking questions and seeking knowledge are crucial for growth. Part of being an adult is knowing what you don't know. Fortunately, you have an inner voice, or gut feeling, that will often kick in when you are unsure. The tricky thing is distinguishing your gut instinct to be careful from simply wanting to stay in your comfort zone. The information you learn in this book will help relieve some of that discomfort and empower you to try new things.

The book begins with health topics and covers self-care basics from grooming to eating habits and doctor visits. Chapter 2 addresses money, with practical advice on saving, spending, and earning. Chapter 3 covers home-related tips on laundry, cooking, and cleaning. Social skills are the focus of chapter 4, with a look at job interviews, social media, and general etiquette. Chapter 5 rounds up other important topics, including pets, travel, room-mates, and more. By the end of the book, you will feel empowered to take on tasks, such as making appointments over the phone or confidently filling out complicated forms.

Ready to dive in? Simply browse the contents and start with what seems interesting to you. You can tackle the book in any order, all at once, or over time, but be prepared to emerge a savvy, knowl-edgeable young adult. Watch out, world!

CHAPTER 1

Health Skills

The word "health" covers a lot of ground. It includes what you put in your body, keeping that body fit, going to doctor appointments, and grooming. Forming good habits today is the best way to look and feel your best decades from now. Family history and the genes you were born with may present health challenges during your lifetime. The better you maintain your body, the better you'll be able to fight common colds, as well as more complicated genetic or unexpected illnesses and diseases. You only get one body! It works hard, so reward it by showing self-care.

CREATING HEALTHY HABITS

Good health habits pave the way to a longer, more vibrant life. Basic tasks, like brushing your teeth, have tremendous health benefits when performed consistently. The following section details how and why these seemingly mundane rituals can be powerful health tools.

Hygiene

Without daily tending, subtle body changes may lead to bigger autoimmune, or vitamin deficiency, issues that go unnoticed. Here are some tips:

Cleansing power: Showering and washing your hands rids your body of bad bacteria, lessening the opportunity for the transmission of germs while keeping the good bacteria you need.

Deodorant vs. antiperspirant: Deodorants control odor, but antiperspirants control sweating; which one you choose is a personal preference. If you have uncontrollable sweating, speak to your doctor.

Comparison shop: Economical hygiene brands can work as well as pricier ones. Test a range of products to find value and results.

Dental Care

Your mouth is the gateway to the body, and having good dental practices keeps harmful bacteria from invading the rest of your system.

Daily routine: Your daily routine should include two minutes of brushing twice a day and flossing once a day. Always remember those back teeth!

Dental visits: Semiannual visits to the dentist cut down on plaque buildup and help identify and treat cavities or gum disease.

Pay attention: Be aware of signs of issues like tooth pain when eating hot or cold food (cavities) or chronic bad breath (infection or disease).

Skin Care

Your skin is your biggest organ. Treat it well with these tips:

Washing: Products depend on skin type—oily, dry, or a combination of both. Regardless of your type, washing and moisturizing your face morning and night is recommended.

Acne: Acne is common for many teens, but resist the urge to pick a pimple or blackhead. Picking can make a pimple worse and lead to scarring.

Dermatologist: Dermatologists can determine skin type and recommend acne treatment and exfoliating products to remove dead skin and unclog pores. (See Doctors 101, page 11.)

Shaving

There are many ways to remove hair. Choose the method you prefer!

Face: Facial razors include electric razors, cartridge razors with replaceable blades, and disposable razors. Experiment to find a clean shave within your budget but consider that disposable razors and blades for cartridge razors need to be replaced after 5 to 10 shaves. Shaving cream lubricates skin, preventing razor burn or nicks.

Body: Cream, wax, or gel hair removers are store-bought options for removing body hair in sensitive or hard-to-reach areas. Test for allergies or sensitivity by putting a small amount on your wrist first.

Laser hair removal: This is a more permanent form of hair removal. Research professional laser treatments as they can be expensive and often require multiple visits.

Hair and Nails

Hair and nail care is not just cosmetic. Hair protects your scalp from UV rays and regulates body temperature, and nails protect fingers and toes.

Hair care: You probably have a hair routine, but if budget is a factor, try less expensive products, get a dry cut, or use a stylist in training to save money. Remember that heat from hairstyling tools and hair dye can cause long-term damage.

Nail care: Manicures and pedicures can happen at home or in a salon, but take a break from polish or gel periodically to avoid nail damage. Brittle nails, indentations, or lines can signal dietary deficiency. Report big changes to a physician.

EATING WELL AND A BALANCED DIET

It is easy to confuse eating a lot of food with eating well. Eating well is more about balance than calories. Here are tips to achieve balance:

How much to eat: Most people agree that eating three times a day is best with healthy snacks in between to stop hunger pangs or lags in energy.

What to eat: Your diet should be like a rainbow. Mixing red and orange fruits with green and yellow vegetables at every meal brings a variety of nutrients. Limiting sugar and starchy foods helps with energy levels and weight, but don't skimp on dairy to build strong bones or on grains for fiber.

EAT THIS, NOT THAT!

SKIP THIS	PICK THIS
Cookies high in calories	Gingersnaps, caramel or apple cinnamon rice cakes
Cake with icing	Angel food or pound cake with fruit
French fries	Baked potato or sweet potato fries
Candy	Plain 70 percent cacao bars / Dried dates, cherries, or apricots
Ice cream	Sherbet or sorbet, popsicles made with whole fruit
Prepackaged mac & cheese	Homemade mac & cheese
Sugary cereals	Whole-grain cereals / Oatmeal
Bacon	Turkey bacon
Fruit juice with sugar added	Water with fruit infusion
Soda	Water with fruit infusion spray or drops / Flavored sparkling water
Energy drinks	Green or ginger tea
Chips	Air-popped popcorn, seaweed crisps
Granola bars	Protein bars or low-sugar bars / Trail mix without added sugar
Deep-dish pizza	Cauliflower crust pizza, flatbread pizza
White pasta or rice	Whole-grain pasta or riced cauliflower / Brown rice
White bread	Whole-grain bread

STAYING FIT

Moving your body is essential to physical health, but it also benefits your mind.

Exercise basics: Even moderate exercise releases endorphins, neurotransmitters that can boost mood and decrease depression symptoms. The Centers for Disease Control and Prevention (CDC) recommends 150 minutes of moderate exercise a week for teens and young adults, equaling about 20 minutes daily.

Types of exercise: Mixing it up uses different muscles and keeps exercise interesting. Try classes or a gym, cardio and strength exercises, and find exercise times that work for you. Make it fun by tracking goals through wearable technology.

Injuries: Don't push through persistent pain, issues, or injuries. Always consult a doctor.

BASIC MEDICAL SUPPLIES

It's worthwhile having some basic medical supplies in your home to help with common health problems, such as a headache, a cold, the flu, or allergies. Of course, if you are experiencing serious or ongoing health issues, be sure to see a medical professional.

Be sure also to check that you do not have any allergies to any over-the-counter medications or that they do not interfere with other medications you currently take.

These basics should be available at drug stores, big box chains, and grocery stores. Ordering medicine online should be your last resort as there is no way to check expiration dates and specifics.

Allergies: If you suffer from allergies, look for medications with antihistamines for nasal and congestion relief. Read the labels as some medications can make you drowsy. It can be helpful to rinse your eyes after being outside during allergy season.

Cold: Choose a broad-symptom cold medicine in both daytime (non-drowsy) and nighttime versions. Throat lozenges and cough drops help with sore throat and coughing.

First aid: Bandages in all sizes, antiseptic spray, and ointment are all good starts for treating minor wounds or burns. If you have any questions about a cut needing stitches or a burn needing treatment, it is best to seek medical advice.

Flu: The flu is never easy, but you can help reduce fever and body aches with acetaminophen. Be sure to drink plenty of fluids to stay hydrated.

Hydration: Any time you are sick, you run the risk of dehydration, particularly with a fever or vomiting. Keep electrolyte powder packs or drinks handy in case you need a boost. A quick way to monitor hydration is the frequency of urination and the color. Dark urine and infrequent bathroom trips mean you need to replenish.

Pain relief: Acetaminophen relieves pain and fevers and is available sold under brand names as well as generic labeling.

Other supplies: It's a good idea to keep a thermometer handy to check your temperature if you are sick. Keeping hot-and-cold packs is also advisable to provide immediate relief for injuries. Choose a pack that heats in the microwave or cools in the freezer.

DOCTORS 101

You are likely transitioning from parent- or guardian-guided pediatrician visits to appointments alone with a general practitioner, which can be intimidating. Try to view your doctor as a partner in your health and well-being. Make the most of this partnership by being honest and getting prepared for visits with questions and concerns. Take medical advice only after you understand and feel comfortable with the information presented. If you don't feel heard by your doctor, or if they are not a good fit, you have the right to choose another provider. Also, ask your parent or guardian if you would like them to accompany you to appointments or to speak to the doctor.

Primary Care Physician

A primary care physician (PCP) handles annual well visits and minor illnesses. Comfort level and trust are crucial, so get recommendations from friends or trusted adults. Also, check your insurance website or customer service line to make sure your doctor is in-network, or participates in your plan. You can visit out-of-network doctors, but you might have to pay the full cost.

> **Frequency:** Primary care appointments are generally once a year for checkups and vaccinations as well as prescription refills as necessary. Primary care doctors may refer you to specialists for specific issues needing further diagnosis and treatment.

Eye Doctor

If you don't wear glasses, it can be tempting to skip eye exams. However, vision changes can happen at any age, so track eye health and establish a vision baseline. You can use an independent optometrist or a vision center that may be less expensive. Check your vision insurance website or customer service line to ensure the doctor or center participates in your plan.

> **Frequency:** An annual eye exam is important for everyone, especially for those who wear glasses or contacts. Exams include not only vision checks but also screenings for eye diseases like glaucoma and retina health.

Dermatologist

A dermatologist diagnoses and treats skin disorders. Your PCP may refer you to a dermatologist to treat acne or check moles and rashes. As you get older, regular screenings for skin damage and cancer are recommended. Check your insurance website or customer service line to ensure the doctor participates in your plan.

Frequency: See a dermatologist if your PCP suggests it, but also monitor your skin and any freckles or moles that change shape or color. Your doctor may not notice changes like you do, especially in hidden areas like the stomach. Annual screening guidelines depend on family history and skin type.

Dentist

Neglecting your gums and teeth can affect your overall health. Proper brushing, combined with dental visits, is important to maintaining oral health and diagnosing issues before they become serious—and expensive—to treat. If you have dental insurance, check to ensure your dentist participates in your plan.

> **Frequency:** The American Dental Association (ADA) recommends cleanings and checkups twice a year. During these visits you can expect x-rays (once a year), cleaning, flossing, and optional fluoride treatments.

Gynecologist

A gynecologist is a doctor who specializes in women's reproductive health. Due to the sensitive nature of exams and information shared, comfort level is a top priority in choosing a gynecologist. Get recommendations from friends and family, then check that the doctor participates in your insurance plan.

> **Frequency:** Experts say the first gynecological visit should occur by the age of 15. An annual visit is usually adequate unless a specific condition is being treated. Appointments include a pelvic and breast exam and a discussion about any changes since the last visit, as well as birth control options.

Making an Appointment

Doctors require appointments for visits, and many providers have online patient portals for making and tracking them. Ask if your doctor or provider has one. If you call for an appointment, state your name and clarify whether you are calling for a specific issue or a checkup visit. Take advantage of any reminder system offered, as most doctors will charge a fee for missed appointments. It is courteous to be on time, so allow extra time for traffic, parking, and filling out paperwork when you arrive. It will save time if you have your current insurance card and driver's license for check-in.

Filling Out Medical Paperwork

The first office visit often includes providing your medical history and possibly that of your family members. Some information is not mandatory, but whatever you provide helps with your care.
Try to gather information about your ongoing conditions, previous injuries, allergies, medications, or surgeries. If you have access to information about chronic conditions for your parents or siblings, you may be asked to provide this as well.

WHAT ABOUT INSURANCE?

Health insurance allows you to pay a monthly fee, or premium, to decrease medical costs when using participating doctors and facilities. Providers do not participate in every insurance company's plan. To get full benefits, research doctors and facilities before choosing one. It is a complicated system with many options and rules, which is why young adults are allowed to be covered under a parent or guardian's insurance until the age of 26.

Premium: The monthly fee you owe to the insurance company to keep your health insurance plan active.

Deductible: The dollar amount that you pay first before the plan covers costs.

Out-of-pocket limit: The maximum dollar amount you will pay before the plan covers 100 percent of costs.

Co-insurance: Once a deductible is met, co-insurance is the sharing of costs between you and the health plan until the out-of-pocket limit is met. For instance, the plan may pay 80 percent of costs, leaving you responsible for 20 percent.

Co-pay: A small fee for office visits that you pay at the time of the visit.

In-network: When doctors and facilities participate in a specific healthcare plan.

Out-of-network: When doctors and facilities do not participate in a specific healthcare plan.

Health maintenance organization (HMO): HMO plans can only be used for in-network doctors and facilities. There is zero coverage if you choose out-of-network providers and facilities. These plans usually have less expensive premiums but are more limiting than PPOs. A primary physician must refer you to an in-network specialist, when necessary.

Preferred provider organization (PPO): PPO plans give you more flexibility than an HMO plan. You can see providers both in and out of network, and specialists do not require a referral. Because of this flexibility, PPOs generally have more expensive premiums than HMOs.

Health savings account (HSA): HSAs allow you to direct your employer to deduct pre-tax money from paychecks and deposit it into a savings account. You can use this money to pay for qualified medical costs, typically with an HSA debit card. HSA accounts belong to you, the employee, and are tax-free, grow over time, and move with you if you leave a company.

Flexible spending account (FSA): FSAs are also funded with pre-tax money that you direct employers to deduct from your pay, but with limited benefits. For instance, most FSAs do not roll over from year to year. In addition, you cannot take remaining FSA money if you leave a company.

EVERYONE NEEDS INSURANCE

Don't make the mistake of assuming you don't need insurance because you are young and without chronic health issues. Unexpected events, like sports injuries and car accidents, occur daily. Insurance offers peace of mind in case of an unexpected health setback. Some states require adults to have health insurance, so be sure to check your local laws.

→ Many full-time employers offer health insurance, with premiums deducted from your paycheck.

→ These plans can be cost-effective for you because the employer gets a better rate and/or contributes to the cost.

→ Insurance can also be purchased through government-sponsored marketplaces or directly through an insurance company.

CHECKLIST

This chapter covered many topics. Here are your main takeaways:

☐ Caring for your body and hair has health benefits.

☐ Inexpensive products and treatments can be effective.

☐ Your comfort level and insurance participation are important when choosing doctors.

☐ Good oral hygiene includes semiannual dental visits and diligent brushing and flossing.

☐ Plan annual visits to your primary care physician, eye doctor, and gynecologist, if applicable.

☐ Choose healthier alternatives to sugary and fatty foods.

☐ Doctors usually make appointments by phone and charge fees for missed appointments.

☐ Health insurance is complicated but necessary to protect you in case of emergency.

CHAPTER 2

Money Skills

Learning to be responsible with money is a big part of becoming an adult. In this chapter, you'll learn money basics, like handling paychecks, and about the different types of bank and retirement accounts. You'll also get tips on building credit, keeping a budget, and saving for an emergency. Money is a complicated topic, but putting simple tips into action can help you feel more confident when making financial decisions now and in the future.

MAKING MONEY

You may already have a part-time or full-time job. Part-time jobs can offer not only the ability to earn money but also the opportunity to learn new skills, practice time management, and build interpersonal skills. The following are some practical tips for finding jobs and getting paid.

Get a Part-Time Job

Here are some tips to make your job search easier:

Who is hiring: Popular part-time jobs can be found at coffee shops, stores, and gyms, and youth recreation programs.

Considerations: Things to consider when looking for a job include: location and transportation needs, if the hours fit your schedule, or if added perks, like discounts or tips, are included.

Applying: Applications can be completed online or in person. For either type of application, you will need contact information, experience or skills (if any), and a reference that is not a family member. Make sure email addresses are professional without nicknames or trendy terms.

Work permits: Many states require a work permit for anyone under 18 years old. If you need a work permit, it can be obtained from either your school or the state government website. Your guidance counselor, parent, guardian, or employer can help. Most permits are only issued once you have a job offer as proof that you meet the state's employment criteria.

Parent/guardian permission: When applying for jobs, and especially a work permit, adult permission is critical. Discuss scheduling, types of jobs, and transportation, if needed, before starting the job search.

Get recommendations: Almost as important as talking to an adult, checking with friends to see where they work and what the environment is like will save time and help avoid a mismatch.

Hobbies and interests: Give yourself a possible advantage over other applicants by applying for jobs in areas where you have interest or specialized experience. If you are an equestrian, apply for a job at the stables. A musician might try for a job in a music store, for instance.

Summer jobs: Make sure you are aware of dates for vacations, camps, sports practices, or other commitments that will require time off. Employers may not ask for this in the interview but certainly will want it once you are hired.

Start Your Own Business

If schedules and transportation are issues, maybe entrepreneurship is the answer. Here are some tips on how to take a hobby or talent and turn it into profit:

Provide services: People are often willing to pay for services that save them time. Babysitting, mowing lawns, dog walking, shoveling snow, and tutoring are all flexible jobs at a fixed rate. (See What to charge, page 25.)

Provide goods: Many people would prefer to buy something handmade over a commercial offering. Baking, jewelry making, knitting, or crocheting are useful skills for producing goods to sell.

Finding buyers/clients: Start small with family and friends, then expand to local fairs or festivals. Use your social media accounts to get the word out. Try posting videos on your accounts, and use hashtags to gain followers.

Online marketplaces: Websites like eBay and Etsy let you sell items online and set up a virtual store. The sites collect a fee for listing and selling items, so make sure to read all the rules and factor shipping into your overall costs.

Use caution: When you are marketing goods, you are marketing yourself, so use caution. Create an email account dedicated to the business. Use an image promoting your product or service as the profile picture for any business social media account, not your picture. An adult should work with you on setting up the business and have access to all email and social media. To exchange goods, always meet in a public place, preferably with a trusted adult. If providing a service, take someone with you to assess the environment and meet the client first before agreeing to work for them.

What to charge: This is a tricky area and depends on the goods or service provided and where you live. Many times, customers will have an idea of what they're willing to pay, and you can accept or negotiate. If not, check out your competition and use their pricing as a basis. If you're winging it, cover your costs, if any, and then add extra for profit. Prepare to negotiate, but never sell yourself short!

PAYCHECKS 101

Nothing is better than receiving a paycheck for your work. Payment can come in many forms and varying frequency (once a week, once a month, etc.). Here is information about paychecks and getting paid:

Paid on the books: This generally means that your employer is reporting all payments to the Internal Revenue Service (IRS), making both of you responsible for taxes owed. This can include hourly wages, tips, and bonuses in the form of a W-2 or 1099. (See Filing Taxes, page 28.)

Paid off the books: This refers to payment not reported to the IRS by employers. This is an acceptable practice only if you're earning less than the federal minimum for reporting income. Check with an adult about whether you need to report your earnings. Even if the employer doesn't, you might be responsible for reporting your earnings.

Paychecks: Paychecks cover hours worked during a certain period of time, also called a pay period. Those dates should be clearly stated on your check in addition to the number of hours worked, gross pay (your earnings before taxes are deducted), and net pay (what you receive after tax deductions).

Taxes: The government deducts taxes from every paycheck. Federal taxes, state taxes (based on where you live), and social security tax (paid into retirement benefits) will be marked on your paycheck as deductions. It can be surprising to see taxes taken out of your pay for the first time, but it is part of being a citizen.

Direct deposit: Many employers offer to deposit paychecks into your bank account as a service. This means you receive your money faster than getting a paper paycheck and depositing it yourself. To set up direct deposit, you will need the routing number and account number of your bank account. You can find these written on the bottom of your personal check or in your online checking account or banking app.

Cash or cashless app payments: Some payments for goods, services, and tips may come in the form of cash or by cashless app. Transfer these payments to a bank account for safety and accurate accounting. Depending on the amount you receive, you may have to report taxes on money received through these apps, so ask an adult to be sure.

FILING TAXES

U.S. citizens pay taxes to fund national and local services. The federal IRS website lists income minimums for filing taxes on April 15th every year. Reading the following tips, and discussing them with a trusted adult, will make filing taxes less intimidating.

W-2 form: This form is used by employers to report your annual income and all the taxes that have been deducted. As of this date, if you earned less than $600 in a calendar year, then filing a W-2 form is not necessary. If you have earned over $600 and haven't received a W-2 by February 1, contact your employer.

1099 form: This form documents income that has not had taxes deducted. Contractors or freelancers fill out this form. The lack of deductions means you will likely owe money to your state and/or the IRS. Legally, businesses must send a 1099 by January 31st to anyone earning more than $600.

Other forms: Any mail or online statements marked "Tax Document" must be filed with the IRS. This could be interest earned on stocks, money earned from the sale of stocks, or unemployment income.

Filing: There are websites offering free filing, but any income, other than a W-2 status, complicates the process and may incur a fee. This fee is usually less than hiring a professional to file for you.

Dependent status: If you are single and someone else pays for more than half of your expenses (food, education, housing, car, etc.), then you are a dependent. You can still file your own taxes but must check the box on the form that asks if someone can claim you as a dependent.

Refund vs. owing: The IRS has a formula to determine if you overpaid or underpaid taxes during the year. After calculations, you may receive a refund from your state and/or the IRS. If you have 1099 income or a shortage of deductions, it may mean you owe money to your state and/or the IRS. Any money you owe and the accompanying forms must be postmarked, or submitted electronically, by April 15.

Contacting the IRS: Contact the IRS to arrange payment if money owed is a hardship. Do not ignore a debt to the IRS; they want to work with you. Note that the IRS will never call your phone or threaten you. All communication is in the form of a letter. Contact information, as well as FAQs and guidance, are available at the federal IRS website.

MANAGING YOUR MONEY

You worked hard for your money, so you owe it to yourself to be smart with it. Use the following strategies to save, spend responsibly, occasionally indulge, and build credit safely.

Keeping Cash

Cash can be handy, but there are tricks to keeping it safe. Let's talk about cash and how to manage it.

Cash on hand: Keep $20 in your wallet for emergencies. If you have cash from birthdays, graduation, or as payment, deposit it in the bank once you have accumulated $50. Keeping it in your room makes it too easy to spend or misplace.

Keep cash safe: A wallet or purse makes it harder to lose money or have it stolen. Never throw money in your pocket or phone case. At home, designate a specific place to keep cash until you deposit it.

Depositing cash: If you don't have a bank account, talk to your parent or guardian about how to keep cash safely. For example, your parents could deposit cash into an account and keep a ledger for you until you have your own account.

Big bills vs. small bills: It is a fact that if you have a $20 bill, you are likely to spend the entire $20. However, if you carry two $10's instead, it might force you to spend less. Leave the house with only what you need.

When to use cash: Use cash for all small purchases that you can cover. Counting out cash makes you aware of what you are spending and how much remains. Using a debit card, credit card, or payment app makes it seem less like "real money" and makes it harder to track your spending.

Automated teller machine (ATM): ATMs are physical machines that let you withdraw or deposit cash via your debit card. They are widely available in many locations, like banks, drug stores, and convenience stores.

Checking Account

A checking account allows you to deposit money to cover day-to-day transactions. It comes with a debit card (and checks you can purchase) to use to pay at store registers. The money is taken directly from your checking account.

What is it?: A checking account is used to manage short-term money and bills. It is meant to store money that you want to access easily, and the balance goes up and down with deposits and withdrawals.

Opening a checking account: If you are under 18 years old, an adult must cosign the account with you. Research banks and look for minimum balance requirements, fees, and locations. You will need identification (if you have it) and a social security number to open an account.

How to use a checking account: Most banks now have online banking to manage your account without visiting a physical location. Use it to track balances, verify charges, and confirm deposits.

Fees: Most banks require you to set up direct deposit or keep a minimum balance in the account to avoid monthly fees. Make sure to ask about student accounts and know the rules for your checking account to avoid these fees.

Making a deposit: To deposit cash, you must visit a bank branch. To deposit checks, you can visit a branch or use the bank app on your phone. All deposits need an account number to assign it to. Checks require your signature on the back. This is called *endorsing a check*. Don't use nicknames when signing; your signature must match your legal name on the account.

Overdraft: Banks offer overdraft protection if you spend more money than you have, but for a fee. For instance, if you charge $60 on your debit card and only have $50 in your account, overdraft protection approves the charge and you pay an average fee of $35 for each overdraft. Many banks will reorder your transactions from highest to lowest, making you overdraw more quickly and maximizing the fees collected. Plan purchases and spend only what you have to avoid these fees.

Online banks: Online banks don't have physical locations. They typically have low fees or no-fee checking accounts, and many don't require a minimum balance. They can offer early direct deposit and operate solely through the ease of an app or website. You'll need to use an out-of-network ATM to deposit or withdraw cash, but many online banks reimburse you for ATM fees incurred. If you're new to checking accounts and want to be able to talk to a financial professional who knows your account and can answer questions, choose a traditional bank.

Savings Account

To save money with the goal of growing it over time, you need a savings account.

What is it?: A savings account is where money deposited earns interest through Annual Percentage Yield (APY). Your savings account is not attached to a debit card or checks, which helps prevent you from spending as easily. But it's still easily accessible for emergencies or other short-term goals.

Opening a savings account: If you are under 18 years old, an adult must open the account with you. Research banks and look for minimum balance requirements, fees, interest rates, and locations. If you already have a checking account, it is convenient to use the same bank for savings to easily transfer money between checking and savings. Look at both traditional and high-yield savings accounts to see which benefits and limitations are best for you. You'll need identification (if you have it) and a social security number to open an account.

When to use: It is okay to tap into a savings account for special occasions or emergencies. For instance, you can set aside extra money for a vacation and then withdraw that money to pay for it.

How to use: Usually, cash withdrawals require a trip to the bank or ATM. Make sure withdrawals from savings accounts don't take you below any minimum balance required to avoid fees. Some savings accounts limit the number of withdrawals you can make every month. Budgeting the money in your checking account will prevent frequently dipping into your savings.

Other Ways to Save

Savings accounts are just one way to save. The following accounts are designed to grow your money for long-term goals. Note that statements from these accounts marked "Tax Information" must be included in annual tax filings.

Certificate of deposit (CD): A CD earns interest on money for a set time period. You will pay a penalty fee to withdraw from this account before the period is over, but it is a great way to let money grow slowly.

Stocks: Stocks allow you to own a piece of a public company by purchasing a share. For a fee, you can buy stocks through a professional online broker, or using an app. If you are under 18, you need an adult to share a stock account and discuss any risks with you.

Bonds: When you buy a bond, the organization slowly pays back your purchase cost with interest until you recover your original investment. Like stocks, bonds cannot be purchased if you are under 18, so have an adult share an account and discuss any risks with you.

Individual retirement account (IRA): An IRA is a long-term investment account that lets you deduct a portion from your paycheck to save for retirement. IRAs are opened and managed by you if you are over 18 years old or with an adult if you are underage.

401(k): A 401(k) is also used to save for retirement by taking a portion of your paycheck, but it's handled through an employer. A 401(k) lets you move a set amount into savings from each paycheck before taxes are deducted. This decreases your taxable income and saves money on taxes owed.

Getting Credit

Credit is the ability to borrow money from a bank or lender and pay it back. If a bank agrees to lend you money, the terms are better if you have a good credit score. People strive to build good credit because it means they pay less interest and lower penalties, saving them money overall. There are various types of credit and different ways you can build your credit. The following are some credit basics to know:

Credit score: Your credit score tells creditors how well you manage credit and whether you make timely payments. Credit reporting agencies like Equifax and TransUnion keep track of your history to give you a three-digit score, typically ranging from 500 to 850. It is based on factors such as how consistently you make payments on time, how long you've had credit, and how much you owe. The higher your score, the more attractive you are to creditors.

Credit cards: Credit cards have a limit, or maximum you can spend on purchases, and a minimum amount you have to repay every month by a due date. Paying your credit card on time is one way to build credit. Keeping your balances well below the limit also helps your credit score. You must be 18 years old to apply for a credit card in your name.

Loans: Financial institutions lend you money to purchase big items, like houses and cars. They set the terms of the loan, including the interest rate, payment amount, and payment schedule. A loan gives you possession of the item, but you don't own it until the loan is repaid.

Interest rates: These are the percentages credit card companies and lenders charge to lend you money. The interest rate is added to the total amount you borrow. For example, if your balance or amount borrowed is $1,000 and the interest rate is 4 percent, you would owe $1,040. The lender makes $40 profit.

Buy now pay later (BNPL): This allows you to purchase and receive goods and services with an arrangement to split the cost into interest-free installments over a short period of time. Unfortunately, BNPL encourages overspending, can lead to excessive debt, and does not help you build credit. If you're late on payments, the penalty can be steep—flat fees plus as much as 25 percent of the loan amount. In addition, missed payments are reported to credit bureaus and can lower your credit score.

Fraud: Never share your credit card number with anyone, and follow these guidelines: Limit the number of times you save your credit card information on websites and apps, add two-factor authentication to any apps with this information, check your transactions often for unauthorized charges, and keep your credit cards in a safe place. Immediately contact your credit card company if your card is ever lost or stolen.

WAYS TO PAY

Technology gives us even more ways to pay for goods and services. Let's look at common payment methods and the pros and cons of each:

Cash

Cash is a quick and easy way to pay but requires some planning to avoid overspending or fees at ATMs.

How to use: Use cash for small purchases. Keep your receipt because you have no other record (like a credit card statement) of how much you spent. Regardless of how you pay, receipts are best if you must return an item.

Benefits of cash: Cash is convenient, and it naturally limits spending to what you have in your wallet.

Drawbacks: Because ATMs are widely available, they can tempt you to spontaneously withdraw cash. This increases your spending with out-of-network ATM fees if using machines not connected to your bank. Machines will give you a fee warning before completing your transaction so you can cancel. If you need cash, plan ahead, and visit an ATM in your bank network to avoid fees.

Credit Cards

Credit cards allow you to spend a set amount of money (your credit limit) and repay the balance you borrowed each month. Credit cards do not pull money from your bank account.

When to use: Most businesses accept credit cards. Look for a sign on the door or by the register of cards accepted. Some businesses are cash only.

How to use: Businesses scan your credit card number, connect to your card issuer to confirm your balance covers the charge, and authorize or decline it. Always get a receipt, and keep it for your records.

Benefits: Credit cards are convenient and easier than carrying cash. Some credit cards offer rewards and cash back as well as fraud protection or help if disputing a vendor over charges.

Drawbacks: Credit cards make it easy to spend more and lose track of your total spending. Spending more than you can pay back in a month will add interest to the remaining balance. So, if you owe $500 but pay back only $100, a percentage will be added to the $400 left over, making it harder to get back to $0 owed. If you're not careful, you can end up paying more in interest than the original amount you borrowed.

Debit Cards

Debit cards withdraw funds from your bank account to make purchases.

When to use: Debit cards are usually accepted wherever credit cards are. Using a debit card is the same as cash because it takes money from your checking account.

How to use: Always know your checking account balance and spend accordingly. Debit cards often require you to enter a personal identification number (PIN) before an authorization can be issued.

Benefits: They are great for budgeting because they limit spending to what money you have, not your credit limit. If you make a purchase at a grocery or drug store, you can also get cash back without an ATM fee, if the option is available.

Drawbacks: Knowing your balance is essential. If not, you might overdraw your account and your purchase will be rejected, leaving you with no way to pay. Always keep your card and PIN safe; whoever has access to them can get direct access to all your funds.

Payment Apps

Mobile payments, using a payment app on a mobile device, are becoming more popular for purchasing goods and services.

When to use: Payment apps are great for repaying friends and personal transactions. Apps and virtual wallets are commonly used in stores and restaurants, too.

How to use: Apps and virtual wallets are connected to bank accounts or credit cards. When making payments, funds will draw from your connected credit card or bank balance. Watch for fees for payments and transfers.

Benefits: Paying with your mobile device avoids having to carry cash and credit cards.

Drawbacks: Apps can be hacked. Having a passcode on your phone and two-factor authentication on apps will help avoid fraud. Contact your bank if you notice money has been stolen from your account. When using a cash app, never pay unless you can confirm you have the correct handle or a QR code for the intended recipient.

Online Bill Pay

Online and automatic bill pay are types of paperless payment for your bills.

When to use: Paying online is often available for both recurring bills and one-time charges like doctor's visits or home services.

How to use: When you receive a bill, often it has instructions for paying online. Steps may include establishing an account in a payment portal using your account number and adding a credit card or bank information. Most banks also have online bill pay features that allow you to add payees and schedule payments to them. This means your bank will mail a check, use an e-check, or pay electronically. Scheduled payments are generally deducted on a certain day each month, so make sure the money is there a day before the scheduled payment.

Benefits: Online payments are immediate and secure without the hassle of mailing payments. You also get a receipt as soon as payment is made instead of waiting for payment to be credited through the mailing process.

Drawbacks: Any time you enter financial information online, there is a risk. Lessen the risk by only using secure websites, not saving payment information within the website, and saving all emails with payment confirmation.

Checks

A check is a document that tells a bank to pay a specific amount of money from your account to a recipient whose name is written on the check. Checks are generally used for larger purchases where cash is inconvenient.

When to use: Checks can be used to pay rent, pay bills, or as gifts. Many stores don't accept checks and prefer credit cards.

How to use: Make sure you sign a check with your legal name, record it in the transaction register, and deduct it from your balance the minute you write it.

Benefits: Checks allow the bank to deduct the dollar amount from your account. There is less chance for fraud because checks need a signature and identification to be cashed.

Drawbacks: When paying by check, it can take days or longer for a check to clear your bank, delaying payment to the person receiving the check. To avoid late fees when sending checks, consider the time it takes for mail delivery.

HOW TO WRITE A CHECK

Though not as widely used as it was a decade ago, there are still situations (such as paying for rent and repairs) that require a handwritten check.

→ Blank checks never expire, so order checkbooks at the bank when you open your account to save time. Printing and shipping can take a week or more.

→ If you don't have checks on hand and don't have time to order them, you can get a few checks at your bank free of charge or for a small fee.

→ Make sure to record each check in the transaction register that comes with the checks. This record helps with accounting.

→ If you make a mistake, just write the word VOID across the check, and add the voided check number to the registry. Then, start again with the next check in numeric order. If you don't void a check number, it may look like a check is missing and can create issues when balancing your account.

→ If you have to physically mail out a check, buy stamps at your local post office or order them online.

John Smith
765 Dolor sit Amet APT B5
Brooklyn, NY, 12345

CHECK № 0007
DATE: _Aug. 11, 2019_

PAY TO THE ORDER OF: ___Mary Johnson___ $ __715,39__
___Seven hundred fifteen and 39/100___ DOLLARS

PAYABLE AT
ALL LOREM BANK BRANCHES IN USA
ACCOUNT № 001234567

MEMO _Monthly rent_

J. Smith
AUTHORIZED SIGNATURE

⑈456789012⑈ ⑆654321098⑆89098765432109⑈

A. **Today's date**
B. **The name of the person or company you are paying**
C. **The amount you're paying in numbers**
D. **The amount you're paying spelled out in words**
E. **Description of what the check is for**
F. **Your signature**

Money Orders

A money order is like a check but more secure. Money orders are less commonly used than a personal check, but they have value in certain situations. You can buy them with cash at banks, post offices, or from a service like Western Union.

When to use: Use if you don't have checks or if you don't want to share private information on checks, such as your address. For instance, a money order can be used if you're paying a stranger for a marketplace purchase.

Benefits: Money orders protect the privacy of senders. They also guarantee receivers that the money will be there when they cash or deposit them, unlike personal checks that can bounce due to insufficient funds.

Drawbacks: Fees to purchase run between $1 and $5 depending on location. Money orders must be purchased with cash or a debit card and require a stop at a place that sells them, making them less convenient than other payment methods.

SETTING A BUDGET

A budget is a weekly or monthly plan for spending and saving money based on your income and expenses. It's one of the most effective ways to manage your money. Setting a budget requires planning and looking carefully at your income against all your expenses. Here are basic budgeting concepts to know:

Income: Any money coming into your bank account through an allowance, jobs, or gifts. This is the pool of money you work with each month to pay expenses and save.

Expenses: Any bills, payments, or deductions from your bank account. This includes money for living expenses (rent, food, utilities), entertainment, and gas, as well as bills you owe to creditors.

Budgeting tools: There are online templates and apps you can use to keep track of your spending. It's a great way to see all your accounts in one place and set financial goals.

Be realistic: Know yourself and your habits and adjust the budget as needed. For example, if you go out more during the weekends, add those costs into your budget and cut back in other places.

Needs vs. wants: The key to realistic budgeting is distinguishing needs from wants. Food is a need, but buying the latest video game is a want that you should save up for.

Emergency savings: Make a goal to save at least 10 percent of your income for unexpected costs. This gives you a cushion in case of emergencies and helps avoid having to go into credit card debt.

Automate your savings: The saying "pay yourself first" is a helpful reminder to prioritize savings. An easy way to pay yourself first is to set up automatic deposits to move a certain amount of money from your checking account to your savings account at regular intervals. You can also ask your employer to deposit a certain amount from your paycheck to your savings account.

Saving Money on Clothes

Whether you are a fashionista or all about the basics, buying clothes doesn't have to be a budget buster. Here are some ways to lower clothing costs.

Follow washing instructions: Follow label recommendations to take care of the clothes you have and make them last longer.

Secondhand shopping: Save money by buying secondhand items at thrift stores.

Check return policies: Be sure to check these when purchasing in person or online to avoid losing money if an item doesn't fit or isn't what you wanted.

Invest in quality: When you can, try to avoid over-relying on fast fashion to make up your wardrobe. The clothes are not manufactured to last and can have restrictive return policies. Investing in higher-quality clothes that are more resistant to wear and tear can actually save you money in the long run!

Look for sales: Shopping at end-of-season sales can be great for finding discounts. But remember: no matter the savings, it's not a deal if you don't end up using it.

CHECKLIST

I just covered a lot regarding money and finances. Let's review some of the main takeaways:

☐ Part-time jobs during the school year and the summer are one way to earn money.

☐ Consider entrepreneurship if you offer a unique service or talent.

☐ No matter how you earn money, check federal minimums for filing taxes.

☐ Paychecks have deductions for taxes and show pay period and hours worked.

☐ Checking and savings accounts are primary ways of managing money.

☐ Credit is money you borrow from a bank or financial institution and pay back over time.

☐ Credit history rates how much credit you have and whether you make payments on time.

☐ Cash, credit cards, payment apps, and debit cards are the most common ways to pay for goods and services.

☐ A budget is a plan for spending and saving based on your income and expenses.

CHAPTER 3

Home Skills

Part of becoming independent is learning the skills to manage the space you call home, whether it's an apartment, a condo, or a dorm. In this chapter, you will tackle chores (both indoor and outdoor), shopping, cooking, and basic maintenance. This may not be the most glamorous part of adulting, but using the tips and information in this chapter will save you money. Shopping economically, cooking at home instead of ordering or eating out, and performing small home repairs means you won't be paying extra money where you don't need to. When you have control over your own space, you'll feel better equipped to take on other challenges.

CLEANING 101

All spaces, whether big or small, need basic cleaning to avoid germs, or worse, rodents and bugs. Doing a little bit of cleaning each week can keep dirt and germs away. When shopping for cleaning products, read the labels to know how they are best used.

Cleaning the Kitchen

Your kitchen could be a room in an apartment or home or simply a sink and microwave in your dorm. The smaller your cooking space, the more important it becomes to keep dishes, pans, and surfaces clean to remove odors and germs.

Surfaces to clean: Wipe down counters, the sink, inside the microwave, and cooking surfaces like the stove top each time you cook to keep grease and stains from building up.

Refrigerator: Take inventory regularly and toss old or spoiling food. Wipe up any spills right away to avoid odors. Most refrigerators have removable shelves and drawers for ease of cleaning. To absorb odors, keep an open box of baking soda in the refrigerator.

Dishwasher: Although the dishwasher cleans dishes, it still gets grimy. To remove stains and buildup, pull out the bottom rack, pour two to three cups of white vinegar in the bottom, close, and run a cycle without any dishes or detergent. Rinsing dishes and silverware well before loading also helps keep the dishwasher clean for longer.

Oven: Spills happen in the oven and get baked on, making them harder to remove. Some ovens are self-cleaning, which involves heating the oven at extremely high temperatures to remove grime, so follow all directions in the manual. For smaller messes, use oven spray and a sponge.

Appliances: Appliances like air fryers and toasters need attention, too. Use liners or foil in the fryer, Crock-Pot, or toaster oven for easy cleanup. The toaster has a removable tray that should be emptied of crumbs every few weeks.

Types of cleaners: Different kitchen messes call for different cleaners. Counters and stove tops need a gentle cleaner that won't scratch. Use dish soap for hand-washing dishes and dishwasher detergent for the dishwasher. Do not mix these two up! Disinfectant spray and wipes kill germs, but be careful not to put food on freshly disinfected surfaces.

Clean as you go: There is no set rule for how often to clean the kitchen, but the best strategy is to clean as you go. If you see stains, wipe them up. At least once a month, check your appliances and clean any grime or buildup.

WASH THOSE DISHES!

If you don't have a dishwasher, here are some tips for getting dishes, utensils, and cookware clean.

→ Fill the sink with hot water and add the dirty dishes. Hot water kills germs and loosens cooked-on food.

→ Use dish soap with a built-in grease cutter.

→ Let stubborn stains soak overnight, if needed.

→ Use a dish sponge to wash dishes, starting from the least greasy (glasses and silverware) to the greasiest (cookware). Be sure to use a soft sponge for nonstick cookware.

→ Dry dishes with a clean towel or leave them in a countertop dish rack to air-dry.

→ Place dish sponges in the top rack of the dishwasher to clean and remove odor.

Cleaning the Bathroom

Because most bathrooms get warm, they are the perfect breeding ground for germs, mold, and mildew. Follow these tips to keep your bathroom clean:

Surfaces to clean: Germs collect on surfaces when you brush your teeth or use the toilet, so disinfectants are key. Clean all surfaces, including sinks, counters, floors, tub and tiles, and the toilet. Don't use the same cloth/wipe to clean multiple surfaces or you are just spreading the dirt and germs around.

Toilet: This is the least popular of all chores, but an important one. If you don't clean the toilet regularly, not only do germs spread but plumbing issues from bacteria can occur. Always wear gloves and use a toilet brush and spray to reach the entire bowl.

Tub or shower: Not only do tubs and showers have germs, but they are also susceptible to mold and mildew between the tiles. Prevent this by using a daily shower spray and also scrubbing the grout and wiping the shower glass or walls every couple of weeks. Clean out the drain, too, if possible.

Bathroom cleaners: Look for bathroom cleaners labeled for bathroom use and that do double duty as disinfectants, which saves cleaning time. Gloves are essential equipment in the bathroom, and many sprays can be used for both the sink and shower. If your bathroom has a window, ventilate when using cleaning products.

Cleaning frequency: Wiping down countertops and mirrors every day will help with germs. The sink, toilet, and tub/shower should be cleaned every other week. Daily tablets for the toilet and sprays for the shower help deter buildup and make cleaning easier.

Dusting

Dusting not only makes your home look its best, it also keeps your lungs clearer. It also keeps debris from getting into heating and cooling systems.

Surfaces to dust: Dust accumulates on all surfaces, including furniture, televisions, picture frames, ceiling fan blades, and window blinds.

What to dust with: You can buy cloths or save money by using old T-shirts, cloths, or towels. Wetting the dusting cloth beforehand traps the dust and removes it instead of releasing it into the air. Do invest in a dusting wand with a long handle to get hard-to-reach spots.

Cleaners: If you want wood surfaces to shine, use sprays that remove dust and treat the wood. Do not use sprays on televisions or electronics.

Frequency: Dust accumulates quickly, so dust weekly.

Vacuuming

Vacuuming removes crumbs, allergens, dust, and, yes, dead skin cells from carpets and floors. Frequent vacuuming helps control allergies and extends the life of carpet.

Types of vacuums: Vacuums run the gamut from handheld models and stick vacuums with a small canister to larger upright models and robotic self-propelled vacuums. Handhelds help with small messes in between regular cleanings with a larger capacity vacuum. Self-propelled models offer the convenience of setting them to do the work for you, but they can be pricey.

Surfaces to vacuum: All types of rugs and flooring should be vacuumed. If you have a handheld vacuum, you can use it on upholstery, too.

Best practices: Dust and wipe surfaces before vacuuming to avoid adding dirt to clean carpets. Use the vacuum's carpet and floor settings, if it has them, to maximize cleaning. If your vacuum has attachments, use them to get hard-to-reach spots under counters and in corners. Empty the canister or filter regularly, or the vacuum will lose suction power.

Frequency: Use a handheld vacuum to clean small areas with crumbs any time you see them, especially in the kitchen, to deter bugs. Ideally, you should vacuum your house once a week.

Taking Out the Trash

Taking out the trash and recycling frequently keeps your house smelling fresh. It also helps keep bugs and rodents away.

Trash cans and bags: Industrial 30-gallon bags are good for yard cleanup or projects, but use smaller bags, such as 13-gallon, for household trash that needs to be thrown away often to avoid smells.

Where to dispose of trash: Some apartments, condos, and dorms have trash chutes for disposal. Others have outdoor dumpsters. Houses usually require putting trash at the curb for pickup on a scheduled day. The schedule should be in your lease information. If not, ask your landlord or a neighbor. Follow all directions regarding oversized trash like pizza boxes if using a trash chute. After trash pickup, promptly move empty bins back for storage until the next scheduled pickup.

Recycling: Your apartment, condo, or dorm may have a chute or outside dumpster dedicated for recycling. However, it is your job to know what is recycled in your area, as it varies from place to place. Check your state, county, or city website for recycling guidelines. If you live in a house, a bin for recycling is usually provided by your city or county for regular pickup. If you do not have pickup, you can always drop off recyclables at a regional recycling center.

Minimizing odors: Instead of putting raw meat or fish scraps, overripe vegetables, or any other food with strong odors into an indoor trash can, place them in a smaller bag and dispose of it immediately. You can also buy scented trash bags and use disinfectant spray in the empty can before replacing the bag. If composting is available in your area, save food scraps in a special bag for composting drop-off or collection.

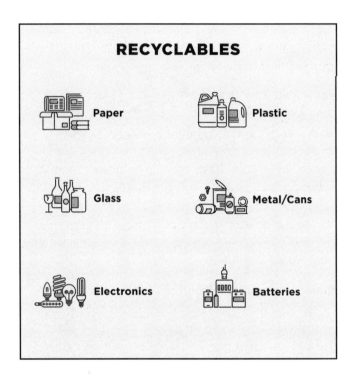

RECYCLABLES

Paper

Plastic

Glass

Metal/Cans

Electronics

Batteries

DOING LAUNDRY

Even if you've done your laundry before, this section will be a great refresher and, possibly, offer a unique tip or two. For those new to laundry, here is your step-by-step guide. This covers everything from what to wash, how to wash it, and storing clean clothes.

Sorting

It's tempting to throw all your clothes into the washer and hit start, but separating clothes into like colors and materials before washing will make them look better and last longer.

Preparing clothes: Start by putting clothes into three piles—whites, lights, and darks. If you are only doing laundry once a week or less, each pile should be large enough for one load. Empty out the pockets as you sort.

Colors: Not all colors are created equal. Light colors and dark colors should be separate loads; dark colors can bleed.

Whites: Whites should always be washed together to prevent colored garments from unintentionally dying that crisp white T-shirt pink or gray.

Delicates: Choose the delicate wash setting for clothes like lingerie and anything silky that might be damaged by the washing machine's agitation on a regular cycle.

Towels and linens: Wash towels and linens on their own because they often shed lint that's difficult to remove from clothes. Towels and sheets should be changed or washed once a week.

Oversized items: Comforters, coats, or large blankets should be washed alone and might require a larger machine. Find a commercial-sized washer in a laundromat near you if your washer isn't big enough.

Choosing the Right Detergent

There are many options for pretreating and washing clothes of all kinds.

Regular: Bottled detergent is available in a variety of price ranges, brands, features, and scents. Ultimately, choose one that fits your budget.

Sensitive: Those with sensitive skin or allergies should look for all-natural or hypoallergenic detergent.

Pods: Detergent pods are an easy way to skip measuring. However, read and follow directions to prevent pods from exploding and staining clothes.

Stain removers: Pretreating clothes with a stain stick, gel, or spray can loosen dirt before washing.

Bleach: Bleach is a powerful cleaning aid that should only be used in small amounts on all-white loads. Exposure to bleach will strip color from clothing.

Fabric softeners: Fabric softener is used to decrease lint and static cling and make fabrics softer. The exception to this is towels, which lose absorbency if washed with softener. If your washer has a dispenser for softener, you can add it before you start the machine. Otherwise, you must stop the machine before the last rinse cycle, add it, and restart.

Water Temperature

The water temperature is just as important as detergent in protecting and cleaning your clothes. Follow the garment labels and these tips:

Hot: Hot water is ideal for towels, linens, and whites. High temperatures sanitize clothing but can strip the color from dyed clothes, as well as shrink them.

Warm: Warm water is okay for most fabrics and colors because it is neither hot nor cold.

Cold: Cold water can be used for most loads to save energy, and it cleans just as well as warm water. Pay attention to labels and know that you may need to pretreat stains if washing in cold water.

Water settings: Generally, use the small setting if the washer is one-third full or less, medium setting if the washer is one-third to three-quarters full, and large if above three-quarters full. If you have a full load of heavy clothes or towels, then use the super setting if there is one.

Washer settings: The washer has a setting for delicates (with less agitation) or a short cycle for less soiled or smaller loads. If you see a mix of temperatures like Hot/Cold, the first temperature listed is the wash cycle and the second is the rinse cycle. Washing in hot and rising in cold can be more economical because you're not paying to heat the water for a full wash.

Drying

The dryer uses heat and tumbling to dry clothes. Not all clothes can go in the dryer, so check labels for dryer settings and instructions. Here are some other tips:

Dryer settings: The dryer has a high setting, which is used for cottons, jeans, and sweatshirts. Medium dry is best for normal weight clothes like T-shirts, underwear, or socks. The low setting is for stretchy fabrics like workout clothes and leggings that take less time to dry.

Air-dry: Laying clothes flat (like sweaters) or hanging them on a dryer rack keeps the shape and makes clothes last longer. When in doubt, air-dry. It also helps cut laundry costs.

Drying large items: Bed linens and comforters should go in the dryer alone. The fitted bed sheet tends to catch smaller items like socks in the elastic, preventing drying. Comforters should be dried on a low setting; stop periodically to fluff them and restart, or toss tennis balls in the dryer with comforters to keep them fluffed. These can all be air dried as well.

Dryer sheets or balls: You can use dryer sheets instead of fabric softener, and they also prevent static cling. Sheets can be used more than once, so shake out your clothes and remove them. Dryer balls are an eco-friendlier reusable alternative to fight static and can last up to 1,000 loads.

Lint filter: Most dryers have a lint filter that needs to be cleaned before each dryer run. Excess lint not only affects drying and heat but can also cause a fire.

Lint vent: The lint vent connects the dryer to the outside or other venting area. This vent needs to be cleaned at least once a year. If renting, ask your landlord whose responsibility this is.

Hand-Washing

Hand-washing is ideal for presoaking fresh stains, as well as cleaning bathing suits and clothes with embellishments. Always check labels for hand-washing instructions.

Where to wash: If you don't have a laundry tub, use the kitchen sink or bathtub (provided both are clean) to hand-wash clothes.

Detergents: There are detergents specifically designed for hand-washing. Do not use regular detergent to hand-wash, as the color may stain the fabric. Most hair shampoos can be used as a substitute if you don't have the specific detergent.

Soaking time: Use room temperature water in the basin and gently rub and massage the garment for about five minutes. Rinse and remove from the water.

Excess water: Hand-washing does not have the benefit of the washer's spin cycle to remove excess water. Don't wring delicate clothes; instead, roll them in a towel to absorb water or fold and gently press the water out, then lay flat or hang to dry.

Dry Cleaning

Some clothing can't be washed with water and needs a dry-cleaning process. Here are some tips on dry cleaning:

What is it?: Dry cleaning skips the water and applies a solvent to remove dirt and stains. That solvent is extracted from the clean clothes, then they are pressed and encased in plastic to preserve them.

What to dry clean: Dress shirts, suits, sweaters, and coats as well as some comforters and draperies are examples of items that might need to be dry cleaned. Check the label to be sure.

Choosing a dry cleaner: It is best to get recommendations, since any time you are cleaning clothes, there is a risk of damage. You want a cleaner with a reputation for good work and owning up to mistakes, if applicable.

Costs: Dry cleaning can be expensive. Dress shirts are the least expensive (can be as low as $2) with sweaters running about $10 and comforters or drapes costing about $30. It is wise to only dry clean items whose tags specify the need.

READING A LAUNDRY LABEL

Machine wash

Gentle cycle

Hand wash

Tumble dry

Wash cold

Do not tumble dry

Wash warm

Dry clean only

Wash hot

Do not dry clean

Normal cycle

Do not iron

Folding

Instead of living out of your clean laundry basket, enjoy the benefits of folding and hanging your clothes after laundering.

Fold or hang right away: The sooner you fold or hang your clothes, the less wrinkled they get. Save time and fold after each load instead of letting it pile up.

Folding shirts: There are several methods for folding shirts; pick the one that works for you. You can even roll shirts to save time and to save space in your drawers.

Hanging clothes: Hang dress shirts, jerseys, and pants quickly to prevent wrinkles. Button the top button on shirts to keep them from sliding off the hanger.

Socks: Resist the urge to throw all your socks into a pile. Match them so you're not hunting for socks each day. Keep any mismatches in a basket until the match shows up.

Ironing

Even with folding and hanging, wrinkles happen. Here are multiple ways to keep your clothes wrinkle-free:

Permanent press setting: Some washers and dryers have a Perm Press setting designed to remove or reduce wrinkles. Use this setting when drying or freshening up one item. Add an ice cube to the dryer on Perm Press cycle to remove wrinkles. Whatever setting you use, always remove clothes from the dryer promptly to avoid deep wrinkles.

Irons and boards: Irons and ironing boards come in all sizes, and the irons have settings designed for different types of fabrics. Know how much ironing you will do before you invest in an iron and ironing board.

Steaming: Clothes steamers use water tanks to heat water until it steams. The steam is applied to a hanging garment to remove wrinkles. Bigger steamers have a hose to apply steam. Travel or handheld versions are more compact and have a vented top to release the steam.

STAYING ORGANIZED

In an organizational system, having a dedicated place for things declutters your space and saves time. Be realistic about your habits and organize yourself accordingly. For instance, if you don't open mail daily, have a place to stow it until you do have the time.

Organize slowly: Analyze one space at a time and find storage and organization tools that solve the individual problems in that area.

Make a list: List items for each space and stick to the list when shopping.

Think multipurpose: Aim for purchases that have multiple purpose. For instance, can you find a key rack with slots for mail that also holds a dog leash? Or can a coat rack have hooks for hats and an umbrella stand? Double duty items are especially useful for small living spaces.

Buy used: Thrift stores and online marketplaces are full of inexpensive pre-owned storage solutions. Also, check Freecycle and Buy Nothing social media groups for free items in your area.

Know yourself: Think about where your clutter comes from. Your habits should determine how you organize and where you focus.

Purge: The more you clean out, the easier it will be to organize. Open mail over the recycling bin. Clean out your backpack or work bag every weekend. Regularly donate or sell old clothes and shoes.

Junk drawer: Every house has a junk drawer where miscellaneous stuff accumulates. This is okay if you know what's there, and it's nothing important. Purge this drawer once a month.

COOKING BASICS

Make the most of your kitchen by stocking it with pantry basics and the right appliances and tools.

Foods to Keep on Hand

These refrigerator and pantry staples provide a good starting point for a variety of meals.

Grains: Pasta and rice are grains that can be eaten alone, as a side dish, or as part of a casserole. Whole grains such as quinoa, millet, and brown rice are filling and healthy.

Eggs: Eggs are a versatile protein that can be eaten for any meal or snack. See page 88 for how to make hard-boiled eggs and page 89 for scrambled eggs.

Fresh fruit: Fruit makes a healthy snack or substitute for dessert. Let underripe fruit ripen at room temperature. Once it is ripe, refrigerate it to keep it fresh longer.

Frozen vegetables: Almost all vegetables can be found frozen for longer shelf life. Thaw frozen vegetables and squeeze out excess water before adding them to a recipe.

Spices: Basic spices like salt, pepper, cinnamon, and garlic salt are staples. Experiment with others like oregano, everything bagel seasoning, and red pepper flakes to find what you like.

Oils and vinegar: Keep vegetable oil or olive oil on hand for frying and sautéing. White vinegar and apple cider vinegar boost recipes needing acid. Combine oil and vinegar to make a simple salad dressing.

Dry ingredients: Flour, sugar, and baking soda aren't just for baking. Many recipes with breading or sauces call for them. Baking soda is also useful as a cleaning agent and serves many purposes.

Condiments: Basics like ketchup, mustard, honey, and maple syrup make great toppers to finished dishes, but they can also be ingredients in recipes.

Milk: Many recipes call for milk. If you don't have milk in the fridge, dried milk is a great alternative with a long shelf life. Nondairy milk and nondairy powder can be substituted when cooking, but check the recipe for substitution equivalents.

Butter: Butter is a staple of many recipes, especially baking. Margarine, salted butter, unsalted butter, and nut butters are all options. All varieties cook differently and add distinct flavor. Typically, you can substitute almond and peanut butter for dairy butter without adjusting measurements.

Basic Kitchen Tools

Having a well-stocked kitchen does little good without the tools to make the food come to life. Check thrift stores before buying anything new.

Frying pan: Frying pans or skillets are good for cooking everything, from eggs to burgers. One small (about 8 inches) and one larger (about 12 inches) should get you started.

Pots: Have at least a few pots to boil water, cook vegetables, or heat soup. A small and medium saucepan, for soups and smaller meals, plus a larger stock pot, for pasta or stews, are good basics.

Silverware: You only need four of each basic utensil (spoon, fork, and butter knife) to start with as long as you wash them frequently.

Knives: You have probably seen a butcher block knife set with sharp steak knives, a paring knife used to peel fruit and vegetables, a bread knife with a serrated edge, a larger slicing knife for melons, and a utility knife that can be used for dicing tomatoes. These sets often come with kitchen scissors for opening food bags and boxes or trimming fat.

Serving utensils: One slotted spoon, one serving spoon, a spatula, a pizza cutter, and salad tongs are a good start.

Can and bottle openers: Invest in an inexpensive can opener and bottle opener to easily open canned pantry items and bottles.

Plates and bowls: A setting for four (dinner plate, salad plate, and a bowl) will be plenty to start with.

Baking sheet: A baking sheet works for pizza, biscuits, or roasting vegetables, not just for making cookies.

Measuring cups and spoons: Most recipes call for exact measurements. Measuring cups for liquids and measuring spoons for dry ingredients will ensure you are cooking with the proper amounts.

Colander: This useful bowl has small holes to drain water from pasta and vegetables after cooking.

Cutting board: Protect countertops by using a cutting board when cutting and chopping food.

Cooking Appliances

Know how to maximize your appliances' power to save time and make delicious food.

Microwave: The microwave is an essential tool for young adults, especially in a dorm. It cooks everything from snacks to pizza and vegetables.

Coffee maker: For many, the day doesn't begin without coffee. A one-cup machine in your dorm or kitchen is convenient, and making your own coffee is cheaper than buying it from a coffee shop.

Toaster or toaster oven: Some dorms don't allow toasters in individual rooms but often provide one in the common area or shared kitchen. The toaster is handy for frozen waffles and bagels, and the toaster oven can cook sandwich melts, pizza, and many small meals.

Stove top and burners: Kitchen stoves are either electric or gas. Gas cooks with a flame in the center of the burner. Electric stoves cook by heating coiled burners. Stoves are used for frying, sautéing, and boiling food. Note that some cookware is designed to be used only on specific burners.

Oven: Kitchen ovens cook food based on the temperature you set. Baking and roasting use temperatures between 200 and 450°F. Broiling is usually over 450°F. Be sure your ovenware can handle the temperature called for in the recipe.

Air fryer: The air fryer is handy for cooking and reheating in less time than ovens or stove cooking. The air fryer needs space and airflow, so it is not recommended for dorms.

Slow cooker/Crock-Pot: Crock-Pots cook food slowly over hours and are great for stews, chili, and feeding a crowd. However, they should not be used in dorm rooms.

Pressure cooker: Pressure cookers add pressure and steam to cook frozen food quickly without thawing. Throw in frozen chicken with barbecue sauce, and soon enough you have shredded chicken for sandwiches. Check your university rules to see if they can be used in the dorm.

Simple Techniques

There are basic cooking techniques that form the foundation of almost all recipes.

Frying: Frying is cooking food in hot oil, over high temperatures, typically in a frying pan or skillet, on the stove top. Be careful—oil splatters can burn you.

Sautéing: Sautéing is cooking slowly with oil over medium heat, in a frying pan or skillet, on the stove top.

Baking: Baking is cooking food slowly in the oven in lower temperatures, ranging from 200 to 400°F. Baking applies not only to baked goods but also to casseroles and meats.

Roasting: Roasting uses dry heat to expose food to a relatively high heat, usually 400°F or above, for a long period of time to create a browned, flavorful exterior.

Broiling: Broiling is used to brown or crisp the surface of foods quickly in the oven under intense heat, usually 450°F or more.

Grilling: Grilling is when high heat is applied to cook foods quickly. It can be done on an outdoor gas or charcoal grill or an indoor countertop grill. Grilling helps sear meat quickly to seal in juices.

Kitchen Safety

Cooking can be fun, but there are some dangers to working in the kitchen. Take note of these safety tips:

Knife safety: Using the right knife for the task is important for safety. Generally, the size of the item you are cutting should mirror the size of the knife blade, so small items need a small blade and larger items need a large one. Keep all knives sharp; sharp knives need less pressure to slice, making them safer.

Oven safety: Use oven mitts anytime you move items in and out of the oven. Place a baking sheet under cookware, if there is a chance of overflow, to avoid smoke and baked-on food. Leaving an oven unattended when cooking is dangerous, so stay close, keep watch, and turn off the oven immediately after use.

Stove safety: I've had dish towels catch fire from being too close to burners. Keep all cloth material away from hot flames, and be sure to turn off burners as soon as you finish cooking.

Grease fires: These fires begin by leaving oil cooking unattended, causing it to get too hot and catch fire. Never use water to put out a grease fire. Turn off the heat, cover the pan with a lid, or throw salt or baking powder in the pan.

Fire extinguisher: Keep a small fire extinguisher in a convenient place in or near your kitchen. Oven or stove fires can be put out immediately with an extinguisher. Familiarize yourself with the instructions before you need to use it in an emergency.

Garbage disposal: The sharp blades of a garbage disposal make it handy for grinding food scraps, but they also pose a danger. Don't put your hands inside the disposal! Run cold water when grinding, and watch for items like silverware or metal that can break the blades.

Bacteria: When preparing raw meat for cooking, clean the cutting board or surface with hot water and soap afterwards to remove harmful bacteria. If grilling, use separate plates for transporting raw and cooked meat. Alternatively, wash the plate and your hands before reusing the plate for cooked meat.

Food Freshness

The government requires that any packaged food we buy carries an expiry date. Yet, the terminology used and the differences between those terms varies. Here are some general guidelines for understanding the differences, as well as some useful tips on food freshness.

Sell-by date: This date is often found on refrigerated or frozen food, and it refers to the last day a store can sell an item. These items, when refrigerated or frozen, can be safe to eat past the sell by date if stored and prepared properly.

Use-by date: This refers to the last day that manufacturers recommend eating the product for quality reasons. Food may still be consumed within a few days of the use-by date, but a drop off in freshness, texture, or taste may occur.

Best-by date: This date indicates when food will have the best flavor or highest quality. Like the use-by date, the best-by recommendation refers only to maximum benefit from food.

Fresh fruits and vegetables: Fresh items do not usually have expiration or use-by dates, so it is up to you to determine whether they are edible. Your sense of sight and smell are key to determining freshness. Look for bright colors, firm texture, and no wilting. Any food with visible mold should be thrown away immediately.

Non-perishables: These are foods that do not need an expiration date and don't "go bad." Even if texture changes, the food itself is still safe to enjoy. Kitchen staples like salt, sugar, uncooked white rice (unopened), and apple cider vinegar are examples. All non-perishables should be kept in a cool, dry place.

Canned foods: Many canned fruits, vegetables, and beans have a long shelf life and are great to keep handy in your kitchen. Canned foods should be stored in a cool, dry place and refrigerated once opened.

Frozen foods: Did you know that frozen fruits and vegetables are often cheaper than the fresh equivalent and just as good for you? They are frozen shortly after harvesting which locks in their goodness, including health-boosting vitamins and minerals.

COOKING SKILLS

Cooking is like any other skill. The more solid your foundation, the easier it gets to build on the basics. Practice the following basics, and you will be ready to tackle more complex meals:

Boiling Water

Boiling water is a skill you will use to cook pasta, eggs, mac & cheese, and rice, as well as soften potatoes and raw vegetables.

1. Fill a medium pot with water according to recipe recommendations. Always measure water; don't guesstimate.

2. Don't overfill the pot, but make sure you have enough water to cover ingredients and account for some evaporation as the water heats.

3. Turn the burner on high heat and cover the pot with a lid.

4. Monitor the pot for overflow or spilling; reduce the heat if necessary.

5. When large bubbles roll in the water, it is boiling.

6. Reduce the heat and follow the cooking directions.

Making a Hard-Boiled Egg

Hard-boiled eggs are the perfect snack and are great sliced on salads. Here are tips for making the perfect hard-boiled egg:

1. Place eggs in a medium pot.

2. Add water until it covers the eggs, plus another inch.

3. Place the pot over medium heat until the water boils. (See Boiling Water, page 87.)

4. Turn off the burner and cover the pot with a lid.

5. Leave the eggs in the hot water for about 15 minutes.

6. Drain the hot water from the pot and fill it with cold water.

7. Leave the eggs in the cold water for about 20 minutes.

8. Drain, transfer the eggs to a container, and store them in the refrigerator for no more than seven days.

Scrambled Eggs/Omelets

Eggs are one of the most versatile kitchen staples. Make scrambled eggs for breakfast or add vegetables and meat for a hearty omelet any time of day.

1. Crack two eggs per person into a bowl.

2. Add a splash of milk for each egg, and stir until mixed.

3. Coat a medium frying pan with butter or nonstick cooking spray.

4. Chop the vegetables or meat if you're making omelets and set aside.

5. Pour the egg mixture into the pan over medium heat.

6. When the edges of the eggs start to harden, use a spatula to gently lift the eggs away from the sides of the pan.

7. **Omelet:** Add ingredients when the middle is still liquid. Use a spatula to fold one side of the eggs over the other, and continue cooking until the eggs are solid and slightly browned on both sides.

8. **Scrambled:** Use a spatula to break the eggs into bite-sized pieces, then cook until fluffy.

Making Pasta

Pasta's versatility makes it a staple of most diets. Use about four quarts of water for every one pound of pasta.

1. Fill a medium pot with water until it's half to three quarters full, and bring it to a boil.

2. Add pasta (2 ounces per serving). Use the total ounces in the box as a guide.

3. Add two shakes of salt to the water and stir. If cooking spaghetti, wait for the pasta to soften, then push it down until submerged.

4. Check the pasta box for the cooking time, which is usually between 7 and 10 minutes.

5. Place a colander in the sink and stir the pasta every couple of minutes.

6. When the time is up, carefully scoop out a noodle, cool, and sample.

7. If it tastes done, use oven mitts to drain the pot into the colander and then pour a little cold water on the pasta.

8. Once drained, place the pasta in the pot and add the sauce.

Sautéing Ground Meat

Ground beef, turkey, or chicken makes a great main ingredient in tacos, or added to pasta. Here are tips for cooking ground meat:

1. For 1 pound of meat, use a medium frying pan.

2. Add the meat to the pan and cook over medium heat.

3. Use a spatula to break the meat into small pieces.

4. Stir with a spatula occasionally, watching for pink areas.

5. While the meat is cooking, put tin foil in the bottom of a small bowl.

6. When the meat is browned, take the pan off the heat.

7. Use a spatula to push the meat to one side of the pan, and tilt the pan slightly so the grease empties into the foil-lined bowl.

8. Wait for the grease to harden (usually over-night) in the foil; ball up the foil, watching for any remaining liquid; remove the foil from the bowl; and throw it in the trash.

HOME SAFETY

You don't have to be living independently to benefit from basic safety tips. These tips can help you whether you're living at home or on your own:

Smoke detector: Property managers or owners are responsible for installing smoke detectors in all residences and hotels in every state. As a renter, you must verify they are present and working. Smoke alarms have test buttons to verify the battery is good. The fire department recommends changing the batteries when you're adjusting clocks for daylight savings to remind yourself.

Carbon monoxide detector: Property managers or owners are responsible for installing carbon monoxide detectors in all residences in every state. As a renter, you must verify they are present and working. They have test buttons to verify the battery is good. Change the batteries when you're adjusting clocks for daylight savings time to remind yourself.

Fire extinguisher: Fire extinguishers are designed for different kinds of fires. Types A, B, and C are typically for the home. Keep at least a Class B extinguisher in the home near the kitchen and only use it for small, contained fires like in a pan or wastebasket. For all other fires, call 911.

Flashlight: Having a flashlight with fresh batteries is essential in a power outage. Don't rely on the flashlight app on your phone as it might not be charged in an emergency.

Emergency plan: Discuss with housemates how to escape in an emergency. Agree on a central meeting spot once you exit the home.

Emergency numbers: Dialing 911 will connect you with a central dispatcher for fire and rescue. Research local non-emergency numbers for the following: to report non-life-threatening issues, for poison control in case a person or a pet ingests toxins, and for the local power company. You should also have the number for the landlord, if applicable.

Water alarms: Water alarms alert you to water overflow and flooding. Place them behind toilets, near the hot water heater, or anywhere that is prone to excess water.

FIX-IT SKILLS

Performing maintenance and minor repairs yourself will save you money and time. The following are minor repairs you can tackle, as well as the tools you will need. When in doubt, always call an adult or a professional to assess the situation and plan.

Basic Tools

A basic toolbox is handy whether you're living at home, in a dorm, or in your own apartment. Here are suggestions for tools to have on hand:

Hammer: Use hammers for hanging pictures, assembling furniture, and removing nails.

Screwdrivers: Buy a screwdriver set with various tips designed for specific screws.

Pliers: Pliers are great as grippers or for twisting wire or metal.

Wrench: There are several types of wrenches, but an open wrench is most popular. Small Allen wrenches often come with self-assembly furniture.

Large scissors: Use heavy-duty scissors to open packages or cut tape.

Duct tape: Duct tape is a strong, sticky tape that can remove lint, plug a hole in a hose, or cover a tear in a window screen.

Super glue: Use this strong glue to mend breaks in fragile items or for projects that need a strong adhesive. Don't let it touch your hands, clothing, or surfaces.

Painter's tape: This blue tape is great for putting on walls and surfaces that you don't want to damage.

Plumber's tape: This white Teflon tape is specifically designed for water pipes and can be used to cover a pipe leak until a professional plumber can get there to repair it.

Tape measure: From measuring room dimensions to hanging pictures, a tape measure is essential.

Change a Lightbulb

Always have a supply of extra lightbulbs of various wattages on hand. They are very fragile, so use caution when handling.

1. Make sure to turn off the light first. Lightly touch the bulb to ensure it is not too hot to handle. When cool to touch, unscrew the lightbulb.

2. Read the wattage on top of the old bulb, and be sure the replacement bulb matches or doesn't exceed that wattage.

3. If the bulb is a regular incandescent, you can throw it away, but if the bulb is broken, wrap it in paper or plastic first. LED and fluorescent bulbs shouldn't go to landfills. Check your recycling

rules to see if bulbs can be added with other re-cycling or need to be taken to a recycling center.

4. Screw the new bulb into the lamp or fixture and turn it on.

Hang a Picture

Nothing makes a place feel more like home than wall art. Here's everything you need to spruce up your walls!

1. Select a wall and measure the width with a tape measure.

2. Inspect the back of the picture for hooks or wire already in place for hanging, or buy a hanging kit from the hardware store.

3. Hold the picture up to the wall using the wall measurement as a guide. When it looks centered, take a pencil or piece of painter's tape and mark the top of frame.

4. Remove the picture and measure the distance between the top of the frame and the hanging hardware. Then measure down the same distance from the mark on the wall. This will be the spot for the nail or screw. If renting or in a dorm, con-sider clean-release adhesive hooks.

5. Nails are fine for pictures weighing five pounds or less. Larger pictures need sturdier screws or nails.

6. Attach hanging hardware to the nail, screw, or hook, and step back to check alignment. Adjust as necessary.

Repair a Hole

If you are renting, holes in the wall usually need to be repaired to get your deposit back. However, if the hole is larger than a business card, you probably need a professional.

1. For nail and screw holes, buy spackling paste and a putty knife at the hardware or a big-box store.

2. For small holes, dip your index finger into the putty and scoop out enough to cover the tip of the finger.

3. Add the putty to the wall, working it into the hole. Wipe away excess putty with your finger or a towel.

4. For bigger holes, use a putty knife to scoop out more putty and smooth it out.

5. Once it dries, the hole should be hidden.

Unclog a Toilet

Maybe you've already encountered this common bathroom dilemma. In case you haven't, here's what to do.

1. If the toilet does not flush, do not flush it again or the water can rise even higher, leading to spill-over.

2. If you have a plunger, insert it into the bowl slowly so nothing splashes. Only a plunger labeled toilet or flange will unclog a toilet.

3. Cover the drain hole completely with the rubber end of the plunger.

4. Push down five times in rapid succession without lifting the plunger from the hole. Then, flush the toilet.

5. **If the bowl drains**, dip the plunger in the clean water to remove any waste. Flush again and let the plunger dry by resting it horizontally between the seat and the base.

6. **If the bowl doesn't drain**, keep pushing on the plunger as it finishes the flush cycle. Repeat step 4 until the toilet drains.

7. **If it still doesn't drain**, call a professional plumber.

Reset a Circuit Breaker

The circuit breaker box is the hub for all electrical outlets and power in a home. If you lose power, here is how to reset the circuit:

1. Open the door of the steel circuit box. Circuit boxes are often in basements or main hallways and are easily accessible.

2. There should be labels next to each switch stating what area of the house or major appliance it connects to.

3. When circuit breakers are on, they are "flipped" or facing the same direction.

4. When they are off, they may be "flipped" the opposite way.

5. Identify which breaker controls your current outage and flip it to the "on" position.

6. Close the box and test the power in the outage area.

7. If power is not restored after resetting, call a professional electrician.

> **To reset a GFI outlet:** A GFI outlet has buttons between the plugs and protects against electricity escaping the outlet. They are often found in bathrooms and kitchens. If an outlet won't work, simply press the reset button and power should return.

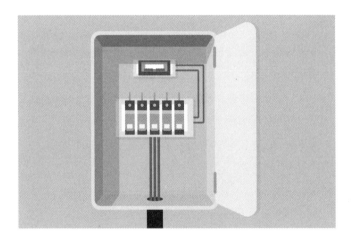

Turning Off Water and Gas

In case of an emergency or repair, you may need to shut off the water or gas to your place. Most valves have markings, but it is your responsibility to ask and know where your valves are.

- If a toilet is overflowing, reach behind the toilet and turn the knob on the pipes near the floor to the right until you hear the water shut off.

- There should be a similar knob under all sinks to turn water off.

- Outdoor water spigots need to be turned off in the winter so they don't freeze. Turn the outdoor knob to the right and find the main valve (usually in the basement) and turn it to the right as well.

- Gas shutoff valves have to be within six feet of the appliance, so the stove valve is either under the cooktop in a cabinet or behind the stove itself.

General Household Tips

These tips may not be in a manual or book but are considered common knowledge by those with experience:

Righty tighty, lefty loosey: Turn to the right to tighten something, and turn to the left to loosen. Generally, right turns "off" and left turns "on."

Hot and cold: When colors are displayed for temperature, hot is marked red and cold is marked blue.

Heat and air conditioning: When you leave the house, adjust your thermostat so you're not wasting energy on an empty house. Never set the heat lower than 55 degrees to prevent freezing pipes.

Extra heat: Candles and space heaters are cozy but dangerous if left unattended. Extinguish both before bed and before leaving home.

Deterring bugs: All bugs hate the smell of peppermint. Buy a spray marked safe for pets (not essential oils) and spritz as needed.

Drains: If a tub drains slowly, there is a clog, usually caused by hair that has built up. Try straightening the hook of a wire hanger to pull out a clog after removing the drain cover.

Gutters/downspouts: If it is raining, water should be running from the top gutter to the downspout, and to the ground. If you don't see water, there is a clog somewhere. Reach out to your landlord or property manager to remedy.

HOW TO HANDLE AN EMERGENCY

Emergencies happen, but being prepared can help contain the situation until a professional repair person arrives. Know who is responsible for repairs and how to contact a landlord, resident advisor (RA), or property manager in an emergency. Most dorms, apartment complexes, and condominiums have an emergency line to report major issues.

Power outages: Nothing is more jarring than suddenly losing power. Always have a flashlight and extra batteries on hand. Outages are usually temporary, but look outside to see if street lamps and other houses have lights, and check your circuit breaker box (see page 99). If you believe you are the only one without power, call and report it to your local power company, then call your landlord or property manager.

Water changes color: Sometimes faucet water can look brown or cloudy or have an odor. Although it may be okay to wash with, you should not drink any water that looks or smells abnormal. Run the water for a few minutes and test it again. If it still looks or smells off, contact your landlord or property manager, and check county and state health department websites for any alerts.

Heat or air conditioning (AC) outages: If you have power but no heat or AC, it is either a fuse or the system itself. Check the circuit breaker (see page 99). If the fuse for the system is in the "on" position, report it to your landlord or property manager, or call a repair person if it is your responsibility.

No hot water: This is not an emergency but a big inconvenience. Water is heated by the hot water heater and then flows to the faucets. Check the circuit breaker (see page 99). If the fuse connected to the hot water heater is in the "on" position, report the problem to your landlord or property manager, or call a repair person if it is your responsibility.

Water leak: Part of living independently is to observe changes to walls, windows, appliances, and floors. Water leaks can be sneaky, and even a slow drip can lead to big problems.

Leaks in your property: Wet items under a sink may signal a leak. In this case, turn on the water and watch for dripping. If you identify a leak, report it to your landlord or property manager. You can either turn off the water (see page 100) or apply plumber's tape (see page 95) until a professional arrives.

Leaks coming from other properties: Brown stains on the ceiling, moist drywall or carpet, or buckling floors can all be signs that water is invading your home from an outside source. This is common in condos or apartments where pipes run from one unit to another. This issue must be reported to a landlord or property manager immediately to prevent further damage.

Bugs and rodents: Bugs and rodents are often a part of community living, but you can help limit infestation. Start by washing dishes immediately, vacuuming, cleaning counters and surfaces, limiting the rooms where food is allowed, storing food in airtight containers, and taking out the trash. If the problem persists, call your landlord or property manager. In the meantime, use peppermint spray (see page 102), and buy and set traps. Vinegar and bay leaves are pantry items that help deter bugs.

Calling a repair person: If it is your responsibility to call a repair person, make sure to get recommendations from family or friends, get more than one price quote, and ask about upfront charges, like fees for a service call to analyze the issue. Know your warranty and if the problem is covered, which would mean there is no charge to you.

CHECKLIST

We have given you the tools to cook, clean, organize, and be safe in your home. Here is a recap!

☐ Regular cleaning prevents germs and allergens from accumulating in your home.

☐ There are many cleaning products and tools designed for each room of your house.

☐ Separate laundry by color before washing to keep clothes in good shape.

☐ Hand wash and air-dry delicate clothing and dry clean special fabrics.

☐ Consider lifestyle, space limitations, and budget when organizing your home.

☐ Stocking your kitchen with basic tools and staples will make cooking easier.

☐ Kitchen safety is just as important as cooking skills.

☐ Check smoke alarm batteries semi-annually, and have an emergency plan.

☐ A basic toolbox will cover most minor repairs and tasks you will need.

☐ Evaluate if you can fix something yourself or if you must hire a professional.

CHAPTER 4

Social Skills

Technology is a valuable tool that makes it easy to connect with people in our lives, but it can also lead to fewer social interactions in real life. Fortunately, the basics of social etiquette remain the same whether you communicate in person or via cell phones. In this chapter, you'll review best practices for common situations, like dinner etiquette, sending thank-you notes, and even surviving job interviews. You'll also get tips on how to balance technology with in-person interactions. As you learn to navigate different social situations, you'll be on your way to becoming a well-rounded, confident adult.

COMMUNICATION 101

In this section, you'll take a deep dive into face-to-face communication. This includes everything from casual gatherings with friends to more formal meetings with teachers, professors, or coworkers. Communication is more than words and includes nonverbal communication like body posture and facial expressions. For instance, crossing your arms while engaged in conversation can convey that you are not open and friendly. Averting your eyes and not focusing on the person speaking may signal disinterest and disrespect. Being fully present in every interaction takes practice. Practice with people you are comfortable with, like family and friends. Try putting your phone away, facing the person you are conversing with, and blocking out everything except what they are saying. It takes work, but meaningful exchanges and relationships are worth it. As you get older, being able to communicate improves job prospects, deepens friendships, and allows for life-long learning.

Making eye contact: Whether you are face-to-face or in a video chat, eye contact is essential to effective communication. It doesn't need to be a staring contest, but meet the other person's eyes periodically to let them know you're listening. If eye contact feels uncomfortable, try focusing on another part of their face, or take breaks between moments of eye contact.

Active listening: Nodding, laughing when appropriate, and not interrupting are all part of active listening. Don't focus only on what you're going to say next. Be a part of an ongoing dialogue by building on what the other person said.

Creating dialogue: Listening is important, but adding to the conversation is important too. Asking open-ended questions or making simple comments shows interest and keeps the dialogue flowing.

Icebreakers: Keep a few questions or conversation starters in the back of your mind. For example, if you're at a house party, you might ask, "How do you know [insert mutual friend's name]?" or "Have you tried any of the food?" to engage others.

Addressing people: It is polite to address people by name if you know it. How you address them (formally or informally) depends on your relationship, but often the way you are introduced is a clue. For instance, if someone is introduced as Professor Smith, you would address them that way unless they specify differently.

Forgetting names: It happens to everyone; you forget the name of someone you've been introduced to. Simply own the misstep, and politely ask for their name again.

Personal space: Psychologists have found most people are comfortable with about 18 inches of personal space when in groups or in conversation. Make sure to give people plenty of space when interacting in person, especially those you don't know very well.

Exercising Empathy

Unlike sympathy, which means having feelings like pity and sadness without identifying with another person, empathy is the ability to understand what another is experiencing as if it's your own experience. Practicing empathy allows you to communicate in ways that others can easily understand.

Understanding emotions: Having empathy means knowing emotions affect people differently. It's important to accept other people's emotions as valid even if you find them uncomfortable or unexpected. This includes accepting your own emotions as valid, too.

Considering other perspectives: Other people's perspectives may cause them to have different opinions and reactions to situations. Their perspectives deserve respect and validation, too. By showing empathy you can learn to see the world through other perspectives.

Ask questions: The best way to develop a deeper understanding of another's problem is to ask questions. This should not be in a meddling, gossipy way, but offering understanding and support. "How are you feeling?" or "How can I help you navigate this?" are simple questions that show your willingness to listen and assist.

ETIQUETTE DO'S AND DON'T'S

Etiquette is a catchall phrase for the ways to properly conduct yourself in society. Here are some handy dos and don'ts that can cover you in a variety of situations.

DO take others around you into consideration. The overarching idea of etiquette is an awareness of your surroundings and people sharing space with you.

DON'T take everyday niceties for granted. "Please" and "thank you" are two important phrases for strangers, friends, and family alike.

DO look to see if someone is behind you when entering and exiting. Hold the door if someone is there. If someone holds the door for you, make sure to thank them!

DON'T think apologizing makes you weak. Accountability is a large part of maturity. When you are wrong or make a mistake, admit it, say sorry, and learn from it.

DO arrive on time! Being late shows disrespect for others' time.

DON'T forget to RSVP. If an invitation asks for a response, offer one in the timeframe requested.

DO greet others when entering a room. If you have not met them, make sure to introduce yourself and invite them to do the same. See Making Introductions on page 115 for more.

DON'T curse in public. With hundreds of thousands of words to choose from, there is a way to express what you're feeling without being offensive.

DO offer your seat to a senior citizen, people with disabilities, or families with small children, if you are able.

DON'T interrupt when others are speaking. Wait for a break in conversation and then speak.

DO say "Excuse me," if you accidentally bump into someone, need to slide past in a confined space, or belch out loud.

DON'T forget to cover your mouth with a tissue or your sleeved elbow when you cough or sneeze.

MAKING INTRODUCTIONS

Introductions don't have to be awkward. In fact, taking the initiative shows confidence and makes a wonderful first impression.

→ If introducing yourself to a newcomer, simply say, "Hi! I am Maureen, I don't think we've met." You can follow up with how you know the host or what has brought you there.

→ If introducing two people who know you but not each other, you can say, "Maureen, this is my coworker, Mark. Mark, this is my friend Maureen." You can follow up with details like how long you've known each other or a funny story to make everyone feel at ease.

→ If you don't remember someone's name but they seem to know you, simply say, "Sorry, I know I've met you, but I am so bad with names. Can you remind me of your name again?"

Dining Etiquette

Whether dining with family at home, at a friend's house, or in a restaurant, there are some basic rules that show consideration to others dining with you.

Before Eating

- Put your napkin on your lap. If eating a messy or handheld meal, ask for extra napkins.

- Sit up straight with elbows off the table. It can be tempting to lean on your elbows if it becomes a habit, so practice keeping elbows off at home.

- Wait for everyone to be seated and served (including the cook) before eating.

- Ask for items to be passed instead of reaching across the table to grab dishes.

When Eating

- If you are a guest and don't like a dish being served, politely decline or only take a small portion to sample. If you don't like a dish once you taste it, eat as much as you can tolerate. Restaurants will replace a dish cooked badly or not to order.

- If someone asks a question, hold up a finger indicating you need a minute to finish chewing.

- A formally set table can be a sea of plates and glasses. For a full table setting, forks are placed on the left, and knives and spoons go on the right. When there are multiple courses, start from the outside utensils in, working your way toward the plate. This handy tip ensures you are using the place settings assigned to your seat: Forming the letter "b" with your left hand is a reminder your bread plate is on the left. Forming the letter "d" with your right hand is a reminder that the drinking glass on your right is yours. See figure A.

- When you need to take a break during a meal, place your fork and knife on your plate with tips touching and the handles resting on the four o'clock and eight o'clock positions. See figure B.

After Eating

- When you've finished eating, place your silverware on your plate with the handles pointing in the five o'clock position toward you. See figure C.

- Compliment the cook or host with specific mention of something particularly good. Even if nothing stood out to you, thank them for their time, effort, and invitation.

- If you are a guest, offer to clear your plate and help clean up after the meal.

FIGURE A

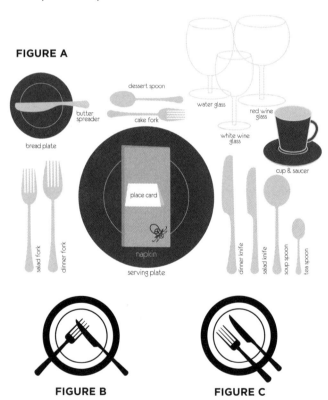

FIGURE B

FIGURE C

RESTAURANT BILLS AND TIPPING

Paying the bill can be confusing when dining out with others.

→ If out with the parents of a friend or significant other, offer to contribute even if the offer won't be accepted.

→ If out with friends, ask for separate checks to control how much you spend. Only order what you can afford, including the tax and a 15 to 20 percent tip.

→ If separate checks are not an option, speak as a group about how to split the bill. Those who ordered pricier options should pay more unless everyone agrees to divide the total evenly. The tip should be added to the total bill if splitting it evenly. Otherwise, everyone pays the tip on their portion of the bill.

→ The tip is based on your total bill. You can use a phone calculator to find 15 to 20 percent of the bill, or there are numerous tipping apps you can download.

continued >>

→ Always round up! A bill for $15.87 should be tipped on $16.00.

→ If your service was unsatisfactory, speak to a manager. Issues like long wait times, food cooked incorrectly, or menu choices may have nothing to do with your server. These issues should be brought up to the manager and not affect the tip if you received prompt, courteous service.

→ If you can't afford a tip of 15 to 20 percent, pay what you can and make sure the server knows it was not because of subpar service. You can write a note on the bill if it's too awkward to talk in person.

→ Pay attention to the small print on the menu. Many restaurants automatically add tips for large groups, don't take cash, or are cash only.

SOCIAL MEDIA DO'S AND DON'T'S

Social media has its own set of etiquette rules, but the basics are the same online: You need to show respect for yourself and others. As social media becomes part of everyday life, remember there are consequences, like losing friends or job opportunities, for irresponsible use.

DO download social media apps to share updates and keep in touch with friends.

DON'T set up fake accounts to post inappropriate content. Artificial intelligence (AI) is getting better at identifying and exposing these accounts and linking them to users.

DO invite people you know to view your social media apps and content.

DON'T accept invitations from people you don't know or whose accounts can't be verified by someone you know.

DO make your account private so only verified connections can see your content.

DON'T take or post pictures or videos of others without permission.

DO report any incident of cyberbullying or inappropriate content through the app. Each app has a method for reporting, usually by clicking on the post itself and following a prompt.

DON'T be a cyberbully, even if it seems like a "joke" to you or if "everyone is saying it." Resist the urge to talk about others. Period.

DO use two-factor authentication to access all apps, when available, to protect your information. Also make sure the email listed on all apps and accounts is current. If you are suddenly locked out of your account, it can usually be reset through email.

DON'T post any identifying information like your address or phone number.

DO use social media to post about hobbies, interests, and topics you're passionate about.

DON'T debate with others vehemently opposed to your opinion. It's very rare to change minds through social media arguments.

DO join social media groups for those who share a common interest or hobby.

DON'T take a screenshot of a direct message or post from someone else and share it without permission.

INTERVIEWING FOR A JOB

In chapter 2 you reviewed job options and applications. Next comes the interview process. If you get an interview, that means your resume or application was well-suited for the position. The interview is your chance to highlight your social skills, show your interest in the job, and ask questions. Here are tips to ace it!

Before the Interview

- Map out transportation, your traveling route, and the time needed to arrive on time.

- Make sure you know the name and title of the person you're meeting with.

- Look professional, regardless of the job. (See Dress for the Occasion on page 129.)

- Print out a few copies of your resume or references to bring to the interview. Bring a notebook and pen to take notes.

- Do your research about the organization. Know the days and hours of operation, what goods or services the business provides, and different roles and departments within the company.

- Do a mock interview with an adult, if possible. However, no one should communicate with the hiring organization except you. An adult can be in the room when you speak on the phone or help write emails, but adults should not have direct contact with your potential employer.

- Prepare a few questions, something general, such as "How did you start with the company, and what is your favorite part about working here?" or "What is the most important quality employees should have to find success within the company?"

During the Interview

- When you arrive at the interview, turn off all notifications and put your phone away. Phones should not be heard and not be out during an interview. Use a notebook for note-taking.

- When you first meet the interviewer, it's natural to feel nervous. Give a firm handshake and make eye contact to show confidence.

- Interviewers often ask about your strengths and weaknesses. Talk about weaknesses that can also be strengths. For instance, saying you're a perfectionist can be a weakness but shows attention to detail.

- Be ready to talk about your schedule availability. Mention any vacation dates or prior commitments that require time off.

- If they didn't disclose salary during the application or interview process, wait to ask until they offer the job. You have time to decline at that point.

- Interviewers can't legally ask you questions about your religion, politics, ethnicity, or sexuality. Additionally, asking about salary history at previous jobs is illegal in some states and never a required answer from an applicant. If you are asked any of these questions, it is okay to say, "I prefer not to answer that question."

- If you don't know the answer to a question, say you don't know but will find out. The willingness to learn shows initiative.

After the Interview

- After the interview, regardless of whether you received an offer, send a thank-you email the same day. See the thank-you note example on page 127.

- If you get an offer, send a thank-you email and discuss salary expectations. If you have room to negotiate, state your case during this time.

- If a week or more has passed and you haven't heard from the interviewer, send a polite follow-up email asking about the status of your application.

Subject Line: Thank you for your time

Dear Name [be sure to include Mr./Ms. or Mrs. or professional title (Dr., etc.)]:

Thank you so much for taking the time to interview me today for the [NAME OF POSITION AT COMPANY] position. It was a wonderful opportunity to learn more about the company and the position I am interested in.

As we spoke, it solidified my desire to join [NAME OF COMPANY] as I have a clearer picture of how my skills, education, and experience will benefit your organization.

Please let me know if you have any questions or need more information or clarification from me. I look forward to speaking with you soon and, again, many thanks for the opportunity.

Sincerely,
[YOUR NAME]

Once You're Hired

Minimum wage: This is the minimum rate, set by each state, that hourly workers can be paid. This amount may be lower if the job involves tipping, but the tips must make up the difference between the minimum wage and the paid wage.

Asking for a raise: Taking on additional duties, being paid less than employees with the same job description, or learning new skills are all reasons to ask for a raise. Practice your reasoning and pitch with a friend or adult before approaching your employer.

Not getting paid: It is customary to wait a week or two before your first paycheck at a new job. However, if you are not paid in the time expected, speak with your supervisor immediately. Not paying employees in a timely manner is against the law.

Quitting a job: Sometimes jobs aren't a good fit for schedule, skill set, or mental health. Discuss options with an adult and respectfully give two weeks' written notice to your employer.

DRESS FOR THE OCCASION

It's tempting to throw on your favorite hoodie for every occasion, but how you dress is a big part of the first impression you make. It can also be a way to show respect for the event and those around you. If you're not sure how to dress, it's usually better to be overdressed rather than under-dressed. For most occasions, it's a good idea to wear clothes free of stains, rips, and wrinkles, even if that is the trend. Tennis shoes and flip-flops are generally considered too casual for professional settings. If you don't own other shoes, choose solid black or white sneakers with subtle logos.

OCCASION	WHAT TO WEAR
Dinner with the parents of your new significant other or friends' parents	Business casual: a simple dress or skirt, slacks or khakis, a button-down shirt
Job interview *NOTE: Even if the job has a uniform, it is best to look professional for the interview.*	Business casual: a simple dress or skirt, slacks or khakis, a button-down shirt

continued >>

Date Night	Casual jeans or leggings are fine in most cases unless you're going to a nicer restaurant, then dress business casual.
College Tour	Casual jeans, leggings or shorts, and T-shirts are fine unless you are meeting with an administrator or faculty.
Formal Meeting (with teachers, campus administrators, or government administrators)	A simple dress or skirt, slacks, khakis, or non-athletic shorts with a button-down shirt
Funerals, Wakes, and Memorial Services	A simple dress or skirt, slacks, or khakis, a button-down shirt. Black or dark colors are the norm at these somber events.
Weddings, Dances, Family Occasions	Most invitations will give hints about dress code. Semiformal will work for most occasions. Semiformal includes a knee-length or mid-length dress or jumpsuit, khakis, jacket and tie, or suit separates. If in doubt, ask the host!

GIVING GIFTS

Gifts are a great way to strengthen relationships and let others know you are thinking of them. When receiving gifts, it is important to remember that the thought and effort put into choosing a gift matter more than the money spent. Give for the joy of it even if you receive nothing in return. Here are some other tips:

When to give gifts: Birthdays, Christmas, Hannukah, graduations, and weddings are typical gift-giving occasions. If you are invited to someone's home, a host gift is polite. A small bouquet of flowers, a candle, or something simple is fine.

Spending: There is no right amount to spend, but it should never create a hardship for you or require borrowing money or going into debt. Determine how many gifts you're purchasing and set a budget for each.

Simple options: Handmade or personalized gifts from the heart are much appreciated. Write a card, draw a picture, make a bracelet, or print a coupon for services, like cleaning or cooking, instead of spending money on gifts.

Gift cards: Gift cards and cash may seem one-size-fits-all, but they feel generic and show no forethought. If you know a card or cash will be appreciated, jazz it up with a mention of their favorite treat or purchase to make with the gift. Every gift should have a personal touch.

Wrap it up: Gift bags and boxes can be expensive. Save wrapping, bags, and bows to reuse, and shop dollar or discount stores for cheaper versions.

Plan ahead: Birthdays and major holidays fall on the same day every year. Purchase gifts ahead of time and tuck them away to spread out spending over a longer period.

Gift registries: People will often make online wish lists or registries for weddings, graduations, or sometimes birthdays. Although you are under no obligation to follow this guide for purchasing gifts, it does give you an idea of what people want. These tools offer inspiration as well as buying options.

Gift receipts: Include a gift receipt whenever possible to give the recipient an option to replace the gift, especially if the purchase doesn't work or is the wrong size.

Regifting: Regifting is tricky. It may be a great way to recycle and reuse, but you should never pass off a regift as something you selected for someone. Add it to another gift or find a clever way to convey that it is a regift, like a tag that says, "It was wrong for me but perfect for you. It came through me first, but is still brand new."

Thank-You Notes

A thank-you note ensures that gifts were received and shows appreciation for the thought.

- Send a thank-you note any time you receive a gift, even if you opened it in person.

- Thank-you notes should be handwritten, not emailed or texted.

- You don't need an actual thank-you card; you can use lined notebook paper.

- There are computer templates for printing a thank-you note, but be sure to mention the gift and giver by name.

- A thank-you note form, with fill-in-the-blanks for names and gift, is not acceptable.

- It's okay to keep a thank-you note short and say the same thing to multiple people.

- If you received money, simply say "generous gift" instead of the dollar amount.

Example:

> Dear Aunt Maureen,
>
> Thank you so much for your generous birthday gift. It will come in handy this summer! Also, thanks for taking the time to stop by my birthday party.
>
> Sincerely,
>
> Your Name

Follow the example for addressing an envelope to mail a thank-you note and any general mail. Stamps can be bought at most grocery stores and the post office.

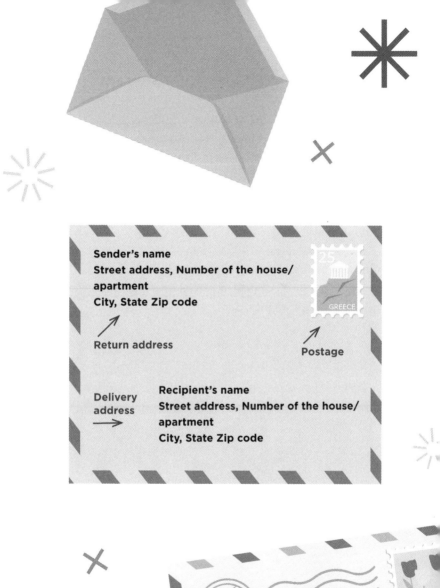

Sender's name
Street address, Number of the house/
apartment
City, State Zip code

Return address

Postage

Delivery
address
→

Recipient's name
Street address, Number of the house/
apartment
City, State Zip code

Mailing a Package

Mailing something larger than a regular envelope requires going to the counter of the post office, parcel-delivery company, or independent pack-and-ship store. At these places you can buy materials for your package, such as boxes and postages stamps, and speak with staff who can help you with your shipping.

Prices vary depending on size, weight, location, and how fast you need the package delivered. You can look online to compare prices and find the option that fits your budget.

CHECKLIST

This chapter has all the tools you need to be a considerate, polite, and generous member of society. Here are some main takeaways:

☐ Social skills are important, both in real life and online.

☐ Communication is both verbal and nonverbal. Eye contact, active listening, and an open mind are keys to good communication.

☐ Good etiquette means being aware of your surroundings and those you share space with.

☐ Keep icebreakers handy so that introducing yourself to others isn't awkward.

☐ When dining with others, be open to new foods, show gratitude to the host and chef, and limit phone use.

☐ When using social media, balance privacy and safety with sharing and engaging.

☐ Job interviews are easier if you prepare by researching the company, knowing your strengths, and asking questions.

☐ Gift giving should be personal and affordable; handmade gifts are a great alternative.

CHAPTER 5

Other Skills

This chapter covers miscellaneous topics not covered in previous chapters, but they are all important aspects of learning to be an adult. Even if some of these situations are not familiar to you now, chances are you will run across them at some point over the next few years. From rideshare apps and pet care to booking your own travel and finding ways to give back, this chapter has you covered.

CAR CARE

If you own or drive a car, you should know that cars have recommended maintenance schedules, usually based on mileage. Other maintenance, like checking for wear and tear on tires, is based on how much you drive. It is up to you to stay on top of maintenance schedules and observe your car for signs of issues.

Oil changes: Oil keeps parts from grinding and wearing down. A professional oil change ensures that the right oil is chosen and that the filters are checked. A sticker is usually placed on the windshield noting the next due date.

Tire maintenance: Knowing how to change a tire is a skill worth learning for emergencies, but if it feels too difficult, know what number to call in case of a flat tire. Paying attention to how your car feels as you drive can provide clues about the tires— whether they are wearing down and need to be replaced.

Battery: Often, you won't know a battery is dead until your car won't start. However, dim lights or an engine that is slow to start are signs of a battery that's running low. If you see these signs, go to a mechanic as soon as possible to check its status.

Brakes: Brakes should be checked by a mechanic as part of scheduled maintenance. If you must press hard on the brake pedal to stop, or if you hear grinding, the brakes need to be checked immediately.

Windshield wiper fluid: Adding wiper fluid to the car is easy to do yourself. Auto and home improvement stores carry jugs of fluid, and the owner's manual shows you how to refill it.

Windshield wiper blades: You can replace wiper blades yourself. Replacements are available at an auto store or dealership. Mechanics may charge $30 or more for labor in addition to the cost of the blades.

Car wash: Regular car washes preserve the car's paint, makes the filters' jobs easier, and can make light scratches less noticeable. A gentle hand-washing using soft cloths and non-damaging soap is less expensive, but occasional professional washes offer deep cleaning.

DASHBOARD ICONS

Your dashboard has tools to alert you to a malfunction or problem. Here are some common icons you may see and what they mean:

Seat belt: Buckle the driver's or passengers' seat belts immediately.

 Low tire pressure: Have an adult or mechanic check immediately for a flat tire or a tire that needs air.

 Fuel: Your fuel level is low, so stop and get gas. Do not continue driving with the fuel light on.

 Brake warning: The emergency brake is on, or the braking system needs immediate attention.

 Engine check: The engine needs to be checked by a mechanic immediately.

 Oil: Low oil pressure needs immediate attention.

 Battery: The battery's charge is low and needs immediate attention.

Airbag: This shows when airbag systems are not working. Check immediately.

Temperature: The car is at risk of overheating and needs immediate attention.

CHOOSING A MECHANIC

Finding a trustworthy mechanic can be difficult. Work with trusted adults to identify a mechanic who is familiar with your type of vehicle and has a good reputation and good customer reviews. Although price should be a consideration, sometimes you get what you pay for. So, if a mechanic is much cheaper than others, it could be a red flag that they are not competent. Recommendations and referrals are important here. Mechanic shops can be independent, part of a dealership, a shop in a gas station, or part of a national chain like Jiffy Lube. It may take some trial and error to find the right person, but if they provide quality work at a price you can afford, it doesn't matter where they are located.

USING RIDESHARE APPS

If you don't have a car, ridesharing apps are a convenient way to get around. That convenience should never come at the expense of safety, however. Ridesharing apps are usually best kept to short distances (under 30 minutes) to avoid high costs. Here are tips to make ridesharing apps useful and secure:

Downloading the app: To get started, download an app onto your smartphone. To compare prices and availability, download apps from two rideshare companies. Follow prompts to set up an account.

Payment method: Most apps require a credit or debit card saved within the app to book a trip.

To book a ride: Log in and follow the prompts regarding the number of passengers, size of the vehicle, and pickup and drop-off locations. You should see a price before confirming. This price does not include tipping, which is optional after drop-off. Most ridesharing apps have the option to share rides and split costs with friends.

Surge pricing: Weekend nights, holidays, or special events, like a concert, may mean higher fares.

Share ride details: Once booked, you should see the option to share your ride details with a contact. For every ride, share details with trusted adults and the people you are meeting up with, especially if you are alone.

Before entering the car: Check the vehicle description and license plate through the app. Then, confirm the drop-off location. This information will be known only by you and the driver assigned. Do not give your name to the driver; the driver should be addressing you by name from the information in the app. If you feel uncomfortable for any reason, walk away. If you are charged, you can dispute it. Your safety is most important.

After the ride: Tip your driver if you had a good experience and your budget allows. You can always enter your own tip amount if the preselected percentages don't work for you. See more about tipping on page 119.

PERSONAL SAFETY

It's important to be aware of your surroundings and cautious with your personal space and information.

- If out at night, travel in groups and never leave a friend alone or go off alone.

- If parking far from your destination, call for a campus or store escort, or call a friend to talk while you walk.

- Do not look at your phone while walking; be alert and keep looking around you.

- Buy a wearable alarm and know how to activate it. Note that mace/pepper spray is legal in all states, but there may be restrictions.

- If running or walking alone, pick well-populated areas, use only one earbud, and stick to daylight hours.

- If someone asks to use your phone, offer to make the call for them, and keep it on speaker. Do not hand your phone to anyone.

- If someone calls claiming to be from a credit card company or bank, ask for the number and call back. If it is legitimate, they will readily offer you the number.

- Trust your gut. If something or someone feels off, remove yourself from the situation and find a friend or a stranger in a position of authority (store manager, security guard, etc.).

BOOKING TRAVEL

Travel opens opportunities for exploration, knowledge, and fun! Booking travel arrangements is often not fun, especially for inexperienced travelers, but these guidelines can help minimize headaches:

When to book: Booking early increases the likelihood of cheaper airfare. Purchasing a ticket at least a month in advance is recommended. However, read the fine print about cancellation and change fees.

Stay flexible: Look for hotels with free cancellation windows, or those that don't require you to pay for the entire stay upfront. Plan for unexpected changes to your travel.

Travel sites: Different types of travel booking options include global sites that search all airlines and track your trip details for price decreases and sales, as well as last-minute booking discount apps. However, not all airlines and hotels take outside bookings. When booking online, use multiple computers, phones, or incognito settings on browsers to evade tracking. Some sites have algorithms saving your search and increasing the price when you revisit the same site.

Travel agents: Travel agents can lend valuable experience but often charge fees of up to $100. They are better suited for big trips with complicated itineraries or layovers.

Before you buy: If pricing is drastically lower than other websites for the same time and destination, there is probably a catch. Read all fine print, use only secure sites, and check online for reviews before booking. Pay particular attention to added bag fees and size restrictions.

What you'll need: When making reservations, traveler names must be provided. The name must match your identification, or you won't be able to fly. You will also need a credit card with billing address, your birthdate, and contact email or cell phone number for confirmation and notification of flight changes.

Age restrictions: Airlines allow 15-year-olds to fly alone. However, most hotels and rental car companies impose restrictions and extra fees for those under 25 years old. Don't just check websites for age rules; call and speak to a person, get their name, and ask for a reservation confirmation in writing.

STORING IMPORTANT DOCUMENTS

It's best to keep all your important documents, such as your passport and social security card, together in a safe and secure place in your home. You should also keep a back-up electronic copy of these, including your license. You can simply take a photo of each document or scan a copy of each of them to store in a secure digital location. While these copies do not quality as legal documentation, they are handy to refer to if you lose the originals.

If you do lose the originals, you will need to do paperwork to replace them. You may need an original copy of your birth certificate with a raised seal when replacing documents. If you don't have this, speak with your parents or guardian.

License: Most states allow you to order a replacement license online, but they send it to the address on the original. There are replacement fees.

Passport: If your passport is lost or stolen, you must report it to the State Department as soon as possible. You can do this online at usa.gov/lost-stolen-passport. This site also contains links for applying for a replacement passport, for which there is a fee. Do not use any non-government websites that offer replacement passports.

Social security card: You may not need to replace your card if you know your Social Security number. In most cases, a physical card isn't necessary. However, if you do wish to replace it, make sure you visit the official social security government website. Follow the directions to request a new card online. If you are under 18, an adult must verify your information. There is no fee.

DEALING WITH ROOMMATES

Even if you grew up with siblings or have experience with shared spaces, there are important things to consider when living with others.

Respect boundaries: Enter a roommate's room only in case of an emergency or with permission. Keep noise levels low especially late at night or early in the morning. Respect shared spaces.

Set expectations: Have a meeting with your roommate(s) before moving in to discuss sleeping habits, work schedules, budget, and anything from the lease that was confusing or needed clarification, such as security deposits or restrictions. Setting expectations early leads to a smoother transition.

Conflict resolution: It can be awkward to talk about touchy topics head-on, but it avoids frustrations building. Be respectful when speaking to roommates, even if you believe you've been wronged. Rely on facts and rules of the lease, when possible, to reinforce your argument. If you can't resolve a problem among yourselves, enlist the help of a trusted adult, a dorm resident advisor (RA), or a friend to act as a neutral party, and, if it's lease related, perhaps the landlord or property manager.

Share responsibilities: This extends beyond just splitting costs; it also includes cleaning and home maintenance. Make a schedule, talk over expectations, and be flexible as you adjust to others' habits.

Guest rules: Guests can include anyone visiting for a short period of time, overnight, or longer. Tell roommates about any guests visiting in advance and be respectful of your roommates' privacy when guests are there.

Stay safe: If a roommate is acting dangerously or illegally, do not wait to speak up. If a conversation does not bring immediate change, go to an adult or the police. Underage drinking, drugs, weapons, and inviting in strangers can endanger everyone living in your space.

TURNING 18

You're likely anticipating this milestone and rightfully so! Anyone 18 years old or older is considered a legal adult. With that designation comes privileges, rights, and responsibilities such as the ones below.

Registering to vote: One of the big changes when you turn 18 is becoming eligible to vote. Voting helps make sure that your voice is heard by the people who make the policies that impact the lives of you and your loved ones. Only those registered can vote in local, state, and national elections. Many motor vehicle departments allow registration when you are applying for your driver's license. You may also register at the usa.gov website, which also has forms for absentee ballots allowing you to vote even if you are temporarily living out of state, say for college or an internship.

Registering for Selective Service: All males between the ages of 18 to 25 years old are required to register with Selective Service. You can register via the website sss.gov.

Registering for organ donation: Deciding to donate organs after death is a personal decision that should be discussed with a trusted adult. Many states allow registration through the driver license process, or you can register online through your state's government website.

Donating blood: Donating blood is a safe, easy process and aids hospitals as well as medical research. The American Red Cross has donation centers across the U.S. There is a screening process to determine eligibility.

PET CARE

Having a pet is fun, but it is also a huge time commitment and responsibility. Here are some things to consider if you're thinking about getting a pet of your own:

Pet deposit: Check that your landlord or school allows pets and, if so, what the restrictions are. This includes all pets, from fish and turtles to cats and dogs. Have an in-depth discussion with your roommates about your choice of a pet to confirm there are no allergies and to get permission from everyone living there. You may have to pay a pet deposit, if pets are allowed.

Do your research: Especially if you're new to pet ownership, choose animals or breeds that fit your space, schedule, and budget.

Buy responsibly: Once you decide on the type of pet you want, consider adopting. Many pet stores and breeders are not regulated, which means the pets may not be in good health or may not have been socialized with other dogs and humans. Whenever possible, choose shelters and rescue organizations that match you with pets in need of homes. Ask about all adoption fees.

Budget for expenses: Pet ownership comes with expenses. Pet food, cat litter, waste bags, vet visits, and grooming are some of the ongoing costs of owning a pet. Find out how much you can afford to spend on pets before bringing an animal home.

Vet visits: Just like you, pets need regular checkups, shots, and care to stay healthy. Ask for recommendations from friends and adults before picking a veterinarian. Sometimes even with regular care, animals develop illnesses that can be very costly to treat.

Food and exercise: Pets need plenty of exercise and healthy food, even if you stay late at work or have an exam. Always have a plan B to care for pets. Your plan B should never assume a roommate will always be there to cover. The walking, feeding, cleaning, and care of a pet should fall on the owner only. Be very sensitive to this if living in a shared space.

Service animals: With the proper certification, the Americans with Disabilities Act treats service animals as a medical need. Also, a licensed mental health professional can prescribe an emotional support animal. Check with your doctor if you believe you qualify.

Pet insurance: Insurance for your pet can limit expenses for veterinary emergencies. Plans and prices vary based on the type of animal (dogs are more expensive than cats), the breed of animal, and its age. Talk this over with an experienced pet owner before buying a pet insurance policy.

GIVING BACK

Donating time, money, or both to a cause is part of being a good citizen. Here are some tips to help you wade through the countless worthy causes and find the right fit for giving back:

- Find a charity that means something to you. It might be a religious or political cause, a group that raises awareness and money for disease research, or an organization dedicated to environmental causes.

- Be realistic about how much time or money you can offer. Organizations appreciate every gesture, no matter how small. When you are short on time, try to donate money, and vice versa.

- When donating money, it is okay to give less than the suggested contribution. A good starting point is to calculate how much you spend on specialty coffee drinks or other treats. Then, see if you can skip those items for a month and instead donate the amount you would have spent on those to your favorite cause or those in need.

- Volunteer opportunities are a great way to give back and meet people with similar interests. If you enjoy running, enter a race where entry fees go to a charity. Skilled in carpentry? Join a group that rehabilitates homes. Sharing your gifts and interests might even help you build your resume or portfolio and lead to paying opportunities.

- Most counties and states have websites dedicated to volunteering opportunities in your area. Use these sites to see what is available near you!

➡ CHECKLIST ⬅

We've covered some out of the ordinary, but important, aspects of adulthood.

☐ Cars are a privilege and responsibility: Follow routine maintenance and pay attention as you drive so you can be aware of potential issues.

☐ Get recommendations for a mechanic that fits your budget and car needs.

☐ When using rideshare apps, share your trip information, split trips with friends when you can, and keep your payment details secure.

☐ Age restrictions and hidden fees complicate booking travel. Always use trusted websites and read the fine print before booking.

☐ Successful co-living requires compromise, coordination, and communication.

☐ Be realistic and do your research regarding space, schedules, and budget restrictions before bringing home a pet.

☐ Giving back is rewarding for you and others! Follow your passion and interests to find the right place to donate time and/or money.

INDEX

E

Eating
balanced diet, 6–7
dining etiquette, 116–120
Eggs
hard-boiled, 88
scrambled/omelets, 89
Electrolytes, 10
Emergencies
how to handle
common, 103–105
phone numbers, 93
plans, 93
savings for, 49
Empathy, 112–113
Endorphins, 8
Entrepreneurship, 24–25
Etiquette
dining, 116–120
do's and
don'ts, 113–115
dressing for the
occasion, 129–130
making introductions, 115
work, 128
Exercise, 8
Expenses, 49
Eye contact, 110–111
Eye doctors, 12

F

Facial care, 3–4
Fire extinguishers, 84, 92
First aid supplies, 9

Fix-it skills
changing lightbulbs, 95–96
hanging pictures, 96–97
repairing holes, 97
resetting circuit breakers, 99
resetting GFI outlets, 100
tips, 101–102
tools, 94–95
turning off water/gas, 100–101
Flexible spending account
(FSA), 18
Flu, 9
Foods
for eating well, 6–7
freshness, 85–86
refrigerator and pantry
staples, 76–78
401(k), 36
Fraud, financial, 38

G

Gas, turning off, 100–101
GFI outlets, resetting, 100
Gift-giving, 131–133
Gutters, 102
Gynecologists, 14

H

Habits, healthy, 1, 2–5
Hair care, 5
Hair removal, 4–5
Hand washing, 2
Health care providers.
See Doctors

ACKNOWLEDGMENTS

Thank you, as always, to my three genuine, productive, and kind children. To Mark, who bravely rides this parenting roller coaster with me, guided by this book's tips and sprinkled with prayers and good fortune. To my brilliant editors, Annie Choi and Connie Santisteban. To my friends and family who were ghosted to preserve deadlines. To the Grown and Flown crew for the constant support. And to my Maryland Girls for never being too busy to blurt text invaluable tips.

ABOUT THE AUTHOR

 **Maureen Stiles** is a freelance writer and editor with a focus on parenting topics and general humor. Her debut book, *The Driving Book for Teens*, was released in 2022 to strong sales and reviews. She has appeared in the *Washington Post* and *New York Times*, and has been published on *TODAY Parents*, as well as a myriad of websites and blogs. She is a native of Washington, DC, where she resides with her husband and three sons.